It's hard to relive the events of Septe
the neighborhood, but Boyle reminds us how a lot of people from
Rockaway stepped up when needed. Read Braving The Waves *for a*
true taste of what it was like on those painful days.

—PETER HAYDEN, DEPUTY CHIEF FDNY

Kevin Boyle has reached into the darkened ruins of the World Trade
Center and the burned-out fuselage of the November 12 plane crash,
and has shown the faith, strength and character of the people of
Rockaway and the firefighters who reside there.

—PUDGIE WALSH, RET. FDNY

I've always known the fire department to be full of heroes. It took an
attack on America to let the world know. Boyle captures it all. The
bravery, the tragedy, the ability to bounce back. The good fortune of
some and the lousy luck of others. It's all here. Above all, Boyle shows
how ordinary people do extraordinary things.

—MIKE SULLIVAN, RET. FDNY

Kevin Boyle not only captures September 11 and the plane crash in
Rockaway, he captures a place, the neighborhood I'm lucky to call
home. Sometimes you can forget how lucky you are, but you can't
forget how strong the people are here. Braving The Waves *is full of*
silver linings.

—TOM MCVEIGH, RET. FDNY

Think about it. First September 11 and then a plane crashes. Right
here. In our neighborhood. Now, that's a book. I'm glad Kevin
Boyle—who lives here and knows Rockaway—is the one writing it.

—LT. BILLY COLLINS, FDNY

Great job by Kevin Boyle. The book is as solid as our neighborhood.
Rockaway is a community that never wavered on September 11 and
November 12. Rockaway is a town that reminds us what matters in
our country: God, family, and friends.

—LT. KEVIN JUDGE, FDNY

Braving The Waves

ROCKAWAY RISES . . . AND RISES AGAIN

by

Kevin Boyle

Rising Star Press
Scotts Valley, California

Rising Star Press
P. O. Box 66378, Scotts Valley, CA 95067-6378
www.RisingStarPress.com

Cover design by Chuck Spidell, Illusio Design (www.illusiodesign.com)
Cover photo by New York City Fire Department Photography Unit
Area map by Greg Tomer, Eternal Designs (www.EternalDesigns.com)

Interior design, composition, and copyediting by Joanne Shwed, Backspace Ink
(www.backspaceink.com)

Library of Congress Cataloging-in-Publication Data

Boyle, Kevin, 1959-
  Braving the waves : Rockaway rises -- and rises again / by Kevin Boyle.
    p. cm.
  ISBN 0-933670-07-9
    1. Rockaway (New York, N.Y.)--History. 2. Rockaway (New York, N.Y.)--Biography.
3. September 11 Terrorist Attacks, 2001--Personal narratives. 4. Aircraft accidents--
New York (State)--Rockaway--History. 5. Fire fighters--New York (State)--New York--
Biography. 6. New York (N.Y.)--History--1951- 7. New York (N.Y.)--Biography.
I. Title.

F129.R8+

                                                                2002031853

To Kathy, who's always believed in me

■ A portion of the proceeds from book sales will be donated to the Graybeards, a nonprofit group dedicating itself to community service in Rockaway. To contribute, please visit their Web site at www.graybeards.com.

Contents

Foreword

There are more than 500 firefighters who live on the Rockaway peninsula, and hundreds more if you count retired guys. Rockaway also has a good number of police officers and emergency responders of all stripes. They've all got stories to tell—great, heroic, inspirational, hair-raising tales.

While putting this book together, I heard a lot of "You should talk to this guy. . . ." Then I'd talk to that guy and he'd say, "You really should talk to so-and-so. . . ." And so it went, until I reached one inescapable conclusion: This book, no single book, could adequately cover all the stories that emanate from an extraordinary place called Rockaway.

I've presented the stories of just a handful of people here, knowing full well that there are more stories to be told, stories that should be told—and hopefully, *will* be told. The fellows I follow here are a fair representation of a bigger group. There are active firefighters, chiefs, retired guys, and some remarkable civilians.

Chapter 1 is partly fictionalized—it's meant to introduce a large number of characters in fairly quick order and to depict what would be a fairly typical end-of-summer weekend in Rockaway before September 11, 2001. Subsequent chapters follow the lives of a handful of people from that momentous day forward. (See the biographies at the back of the book.)

As for my own involvement, I saw the Twin Towers burn from the seawall in Rockaway. The day the plane crashed, I was close enough to the fire to have my eyes dry, though my vision stayed clear enough to see a bunch of ordinary Joes become heroes.

As the stories circulated throughout Rockaway, I thought *some-body* should write a book about this place and its people. Others had the same thought.

I suppose that, because I had worked for Rockaway's only newspaper, *The Wave*, people began telling me I was the one to write it.

Here's my earnest attempt.

Acknowledgements

I couldn't have written this book without the help of people willing to talk about extremely painful episodes in their lives. I owe great thanks to the Heerans—Bernie, Billy, and Sean; to Tom Lawler; and to the firefighters who lost many friends.

I must also thank those who spoke to me about their experiences, and had to put up with me asking the same questions until I finally got it. They include Tommy Carroll, Pete Hayden, Matt Tansey, Monsignor Martin Geraghty, Kenny Whelan, Steve Stathis, George Johnson, Palmer Doyle, Flip Mullen, Tom McVeigh, George Johnson, Sr., and Whipper Stathis. Numerous other guys—a lot of firefighter friends—gave me their time, anecdotes, and information.

Ryan Whelan, Pete Hayden, Jr., Billy and Sean Heeran—Rockaway Irish Boys all—were extremely generous.

The folks at *The Wave*, New York's oldest weekly newspaper, including Howie Schwach and historian Emil Lucev, helped at every turn. E. J. Dionne, Jr., honorary citizen of Rockaway, was generous beyond words.

My agent, Liz Trupin-Pulli, not only represents my work, but is a tireless, insightful reader. I'm grateful to have a publisher/editor, Donna Jacobsen, who shows great enthusiasm for the book, and great sensitivity towards Rockaway and its people.

Finally, I must thank family and friends who read some pretty crude drafts and still managed to encourage me. Carol and Kevin Kelleher, Eileen Carroll, Jim and Marian Dunn, all the Boyles, Alana Landey, and Mark Cannon offered keen eyes for every page.

CHAPTER 1

Belle Harbor

December 1966

They pulled Kenny Whelan from bed early Christmas morning. The house was on fire. Pushed through a hallway towards the door, the 12-year-old felt hot, blistering air on his ears and neck. Then his face felt bitter cold. Nine degrees bitter. There was snow before him and lots of it. Nearly 2 feet had already covered the ground and it was still falling, muting sounds in the street save for bursts of splintering and crackle from the fire. Kenny was hurried, just about carried by the elbows, to a house across the street by men who had come to help from Droesch's Bar, just next door. Before going inside, the young boy saw the flashing lights of a fire truck turning the corner onto Beach 129th Street.

September 2001

The crowds are gone. Gone with Labor Day, just a few days before. The beaches are empty and the summer promises to hang around for another month, just for the locals.

Charlie Heeran, 23, immediately forgets the slow, sweaty ride from Wall Street as he gets off the A train and steps out onto Beach 116th Street. If he turns right, he could walk a block to the edge of the Rockaway Inlet—a blue-green channel that is part of Jamaica Bay. Just past the water lay the brown and gray stretch of Brooklyn. Beyond that, the jagged skyline of Manhattan rises, sparkling like beach quartz. If he turns left, he could walk a block to the Atlantic Ocean.

The red doors of the firehouse across the street slide upward. The captain, in his white hat, steps out and stands to the side as a fire truck rolls slowly out of the garage, a banana-yellow rescue surfboard fastened to its side. Stenciled across the board in bright red letters is the affectionate, somewhat ironic, nickname of this peninsula: Rockapulco.

Kenny Whelan still lives on Beach 129th Street, but he is a long way from the boy who was pulled from the fire in a snowstorm. He'd spent more than 20 years returning the favor, rescuing people as a New York City firefighter. Now he's a captain of the firehouse in his own neighborhood.

Charlie is used to seeing Kenny in a referee's shirt or gym shorts at the St. Francis gym or schoolyard. Now, he figures he might have to start calling him Mister Whelan or Captain, though it'd be tough to call him anything other than Kenny, as he'd been doing his whole life. He practically lived in the Whelan's house growing up. Ryan Whelan, the captain's son, is one of his lifelong buddies. The white captain's hat sure looks good.

A small whirlwind spins Styrofoam cups and loose papers around Charlie's feet as he steps into a moist, offshore wind. Cigarette butts and small clusters of sand bounce past him as he pushes his way towards the ocean boardwalk. He puts his hands in the pockets of his dark, pin-striped suit—the one he hopes would one day feel as good as his old Xavier rugby shirt.

Maybe one day the suit would fit him perfectly, the way the black rubber coat and the boots of the Fire Department of New York (FDNY) used to fit his father, Bernie, who'd retired from the fire department just a year ago. For the longest time, he figured he'd follow in his father's footsteps. He had taken the fire department test, and scored 100 on the written and 100 on the physical. Now, things are going so well on Wall Street that it looks like he'll have to choose finance over fighting fires.

He wonders how Billy, his twin brother, would feel in bunker gear. Right now, Billy is taking a crack at Wall Street, too. He'd also taken the test for the fire department, though his dad wasn't too crazy about either of them even thinking about the firefighting life. It was just too dangerous. There was probably nothing for him to worry about; it looked like Billy would stay on Wall Street. If things worked out, they would be working for the same company pretty soon.

Charlie knows that Rockaway is a place where you can get all four seasons in eight hours. It is early September, but the late afternoon feels like early March. However, in five minutes, it could warm right up, so taking the boardwalk is worth the chance. He could hurry home along Newport Avenue instead, but then he'd never know if the waves were monsters, or if friends would be telling the truth about riding 7-foot swells, or if the color of the water would be blue enough to make him drunk. He could take the short way home, but then he might miss a massive ocean liner on the horizon or a shrimp boat, its arms spread, cleaning the ocean floor. If you have a minute to spare, you take the boardwalk on the stroll home.

First, you have to negotiate Beach 116th Street: a two-block commercial strip, which is the last subway stop on the Rockaway Park branch of the A line, and the stop where summer crowds spill off the trains and hurry to the sand. Try as they might, The Gift is Love, The Beach Club, George's Florist, and West End Realty—clean, welcoming, and fresh businesses—can't cure the block of its ingrained seediness. It's a dollar-store ambience: dollar stores and grimy delis, an abandoned movie theater, panhandlers, a couple of old-man bars, and flophouses. Summer litter that stays all year. It's a shame, people have been saying forever. Possibly the worst thing is that ever-present cop who has blind eyes for everything but an expired parking meter.

As Charlie climbs one of the only hills in Rockaway—a ramp to the boardwalk—he glances at the large herring gull perched on top of an orange mesh garbage can, picking at a stump of kielbasa wedged between two malt liquor bottles. What a shame. Steady, good-sized waves break a hundred feet off the shoreline and, no surprise, the chill is gone and the warm sun washes over his face—a face that everybody says looks like the actor, Matt Damon. Buddies might call him Rugby Chuck, Charlie Tuna, or just Tuna. He is pretty good with bestowing a nickname himself. Charlie is the one who called Sean Hayden "Foakley" one day on the beach because Sean was wearing a pair of fake Oakley sunglasses and the name stuck.

In the distance, he sees half a dozen surfers looking like scattered dominoes sticking out of the water, their black wet suits against the pewter sky. Teenagers or firefighters—who else would have the time? Less time to surf, more time to make money and party. It was one of the trade-offs he made when his other brother, Sean, got him the job on the trading desk. So far, so good. He and his brothers could take up surfing again, down the road, if their Wall Street dreams ever came true.

September and October are the best months for surfing. Hurricanes that rip apart the Bahamas and Florida send gifts to Rockaway in the form of bone-rattling surf. Just like that, Rockaway Beach is the New York version of the Banzai Pipeline. Each wave looks stronger than the one before. The offshore wind helps make the water smooth and the waves crisp, and it looks like Hurricane Erin is going to be generous.

Certain spots along the 11 miles of Rockaway Beach are known for having the best waves, but you'll never get a local to admit it. Locals don't talk much about surfing or secret spots. Hey, there's one spot, when you're kneeling on the board, you can see New Jersey on your left and Long Island on your right. When the waves swell just a bit, you can see—dead ahead—the Empire State Building. *Shhhh!* It'll be ruined if too many people find out.

The boardwalk planks are loose, making Charlie feel like he's walking on piano keys. Like the neighborhood, the boardwalk improves the farther west you walk from Beach 116th Street. It's not entirely true, yet you can pretty well chart the upward climb of family incomes, block by block, for another mile. The first few ocean blocks have some decaying, box-like houses and multiple-dwelling homes; ramshackle wood-frame houses ideal for one or two families that hold five or six. Drab, seven-story apartment buildings along the boardwalk deprive these blocks of direct ocean breezes. The nicer homes—big and gorgeous Queen Annes—are on the bay side.

At Beach 126th Street, the boardwalk ends. You can continue the route by taking to the world's best sand. It's clean, deep, grainy, and light beige—the way sand is supposed to be. People from Rockaway come back from vacations grumbling about beaches in other places where the sand was like dirt or powder, or seemed too much like gravel or was too brown, or there wasn't enough of it to be called a beach. In Rockaway, there's a lot of it. From the oceanfront homes to the shoreline, there's more than a football field-sized stretch of sand.

If you don't want to get the world's best sand in your shoes, you can turn off the boardwalk into the neighborhood called Belle Harbor. As pretty as its name.

Charlie feels funny enough in his new suit. He won't risk being seen on the sand with pin stripes and wing tips. He glances back at three surfers, almost shoulder to shoulder, riding a nice curl. When the wave starts outrunning them, two of them pull their boards up and over the wave like jets leaving formation.

They have to be firefighters. If he were going to have any second thoughts about choosing a Burberry suit over FDNY bunker gear, he'd best grab a beer and some reassurance from his brothers or one of his buddies, Chris Lawler, who'd chosen law school.

■ Two picnic tables are pushed together, end to end, so that the McVeighs, Carrolls, and Kellehers can sit together. At other tables, all within earshot, are the Meades, Dunns, Minginos, and Kings. A pair of fat seagulls is perched on separate pilings just off the boat dock extending from the outdoor deck at The Wharf. Steve Stathis and Jimmy Bulloch stand at the railing and watch a fat man with an open shirt tie his Boston Whaler to the dock below. A young couple sips Coronas, admiring the sunset.

What a sunset. Late summer, the flames have vanished from the sun. It's a big pumpkin sliding down right between the towers of the Verrazano Narrows Bridge. Another set of towers—the Twin

Towers—catch the soft, fading rays and turn almost copper, glistening like two stacks of newly minted pennies.

The Wharf is a no-frills place where you get a cold beer, a so-so burger, and the hands-down best sunset in New York. Because it's hidden behind a gas station on Beach Channel Drive, with no outside sign to advertise the place, you'd think it was owned by surfers trying to keep a secret. Yet, if you do find the place, after you take measure of the surprising bayfront vistas, you meet a make-yourself-at-home staff and a deck full of customers with smiling faces.

Boston Whalers, sailboats, and dinghies dot the clean blue-green water; in the distance stands the majestic Verrazano Narrows Bridge and the serrated Manhattan skyline. When you think you've died and gone to heaven, don't worry, an attention-starved idiot on a jet ski will buzz by as a reminder that you're still in New York.

Beers and finger food are ordered. The kids scatter. Some go inside to the pinball machine; some to the dock to greet a Chris Craft weekend cruiser tying up. It isn't an official retirement party, but Tom McVeigh is willing to have a trial run. In a few weeks, in late September, he'll be calling it a day after 21 years as a New York City firefighter. Still a young man, he'd just turned 42. A whole new career as an executive at a Manhattan moving company awaits.

"Unlike Ralphie boy, here." Eileen Carroll nudges her husband, Tommy—a bear of a man, who is used to comparisons to television's original big dreamer, Ralph Kramden. "No executive position for him when he retires. He'll be too busy working overtime at the get-rich-quick factory."

"I don't need a job," Tommy says. "I need a J-O-B. Just One Break." Everyone groans. He puts up his hands to silence the aggrieved. "I don't complain. If I didn't have bad luck, I wouldn't have any luck at all." His sincere delivery, as if he had just coined the line, gets laughing approval. Eileen gives him the business, but she hopes, for his sake, a moneymaking dream comes true.

When he's not at the firehouse, he breaks his back working construction jobs as a wire lather with Local 46.

Conversation stops as an American Airlines plane from John F. Kennedy (JFK) airport, just a few miles to the east, roars overhead. Everybody shakes their head. "That one was low," Kevin Kelleher says. "Jesus, you can see the people looking out the plane windows."

"Yeah, and you can see they are scared shitless," Tommy says. There is knowing, nervous laughter from everyone who's had a turbulent ride in an aircraft.

"How much time you got in?" Kelleher asks Tommy. Twenty years on the FDNY makes you eligible for retirement. Firefighters spend the last year or so working as much overtime as they can because it means a fatter pension.

"I'm a pup. I just got 17," Tommy says, an idea forming on his face, "but I'm already thinking that maybe I'll contact you at Sony when I'm done. You think you could use a slightly chunky, 45-year-old Ricky Martin type? I still have my powder blue leisure suit from 1978."

Eileen bursts out laughing. Kelleher plays it straight. "Can you sing?"

"No, but you're telling me you have to? I've seen the Grammy Awards. You don't need talent."

Kelleher, the chief financial officer at the music company, says, "Come on. Bruce Springsteen, Aerosmith, and Billy Joel. Tell ya what, though. If you can squeeze into that leisure suit, we'll give you a three-record deal."

As soon as the laughter ebbs, Happy Jack Driscoll at the next table adds, "Sony sucks." That gets a big laugh, too, because it was so predictably Jack—gruff and terse.

"New York's Strongest," Brian King says, implying this sanitation man wasn't "New York's Smartest."

Jack is smart enough to get the implication, so he sneers at King. "Fuckin' lawyer." Again, everyone laughs.

Firefighters, accountants, lawyers, sanitation workers ... it doesn't mean a thing. The only currency that matters here is wise-ass wit. Of course, it's usually garden-variety, locker room stuff, but when you are playing to a bunch of ex-jocks, what better stuff to use? Perhaps the term "ex-jocks" doesn't quite apply. Many of the guys at The Wharf tonight play in an over-40 summer basketball league at St. Francis de Sales, the local Catholic parish. They call themselves the Graybeards. It's a six-team league with roughly 50 players and a long waiting list of guys trying to join these arthritic Peter Pans. Nearly a third are firefighters, and it seems like another third are lawyers and the rest are this and that—a couple of doctors, a couple of cops, sanitation workers, plumbers, elevator repairmen, and accountants.

Steve Stathis, 52, runs the league. He makes sure everyone knows there's no caste system or social hierarchy. It doesn't matter how big your house is, what car you drive, or how much money you make. You want to brag about something, your team had better win the Graybeard championship in July. Winners receive colorful T-shirts with the word "champions" emblazoned down the sleeve and the right, to strut a bit until the start of next season, some time in May. It's silly . . . they know it's silly, but it still feels good, partly because basketball is a prominent thread in the Rockaway fabric. Hall of Fame brothers Dick and Al McGuire grew up here, Nancy Lieberman (a superstar from the women's game), National Basketball Association All-Star Brian Winters, and countless other top players learned the game in the local gyms and playgrounds.

The league is an extra bonus you get living here. People from Rockaway like to say they have "sand in their shoes" the way some people say they bleed red, white, and blue. It's a catch phrase for communal strength and uniqueness, memories, lifestyle, salt air, and an undying love for the place. The league is just a grain of that sand.

Whether you were born and raised in Rockaway or settled here, one thing you can never figure out is what motivates those people who move to New Jersey or Long Island. The last thing anyone in Rockaway wants to get is an invitation to a summer barbecue off the peninsula. "I gotta leave Rockaway to go sit in somebody's backyard? What, are they kiddin'?" This shorthand means that no one wants to deal with traffic, the stale air, and tight confines of a backyard, with more traffic on the way home . . . not when you have the beach and all the friends you need right here. Nobody's surprised when they hear that Jughead McCormack and his wife, Allie, moved to Suffolk County and now want to move back— even if parking can be a hassle.

On the west end of the peninsula, from May 15 through September 30, restrictions apply that prohibit parking cars on the streets on weekends; on some blocks, there's no parking even during the week. It effectively makes the Rockaway public beaches private for those who live on the blocks within walking distance to the ocean. People who come over one of the two bridges to the peninsula from either Brooklyn or Queens are called DFDs, meaning they're Down For the Day. They've got limited options. They can pay for parking on Beach 116th Street, or do the same at Riis Park Beach lot, which is more than a quarter mile from the nearest residence.

Come May 15, there's an inevitable burst of protest. Some call the restrictions elitist; some say it's a burden on those who live in the area but don't have space to put their cars on weekends. The protests come too late to effect a change: the Community Board won't meet until after summer; by then, the restrictions are about to be lifted, the protesters have lost their steam, and they won't remember to raise the issue until next year when it will be too late again.

That doesn't mean the protesters would actually succeed. There is great support for the restrictions. For one thing, there are no public rest rooms at the beach west of Beach 116th Street. More than a few residents who have outdoor showers—a great way to wash sand and salt off before going in the house—have found strangers using the facilities for more than showers.

Some residents say the restrictions, even allowing that they're inconvenient, have actually strengthened community ties. In this part of Rockaway, you walk from your house to the beach. You get a wagon and pile on blankets, towels, lotion, beach chairs, and a cooler. You pass neighbors on the way. You start nodding at them, then saying hello. By next season, maybe you're sitting next to them on the beach. There's a good chance the kids have already made friends and are in the water together.

In most neighborhoods, people drive to the park or beach, or have to leave their community altogether for recreation. In Rockaway, in the section called Belle Harbor in particular, people go to the beach and they get there on foot.

"Golf, and then the beach?" Kelleher asks McVeigh.

"When? Tomorrow?" McVeigh is already looking at his wife, Pat, to see if it's okay.

"I don't care, but Sean's got soccer practice in the morning," Pat says, "and I'm taking Kaitlyn for a haircut." McVeigh considers all this, locks his hands in a golf grip, and nods: he's in.

"Flip Mullen is having that fundraiser for the Special Olympics, so we gotta get back for that," McVeigh says, turning to Tommy. "You going?"

"I wish, but I got the firehouse."

"He's gotta work on his beauty sleep," Eileen says.

"McVeigh, tell 'em. We work like dogs," Tommy says.

McVeigh puts up his hands. "Leave me out of this." McVeigh won't talk shop. Most firefighters are like that. They'll volunteer funny stuff, but they generally won't talk about running into burning buildings. It's easy to forget what they actually do, because they'd rather talk about how much they eat or about the new exercise equipment they just installed at the firehouse.

McVeigh won't help and Tommy realizes there's only one way out. "We work like dogs," Tommy says. "We die young and our wives won't sleep in the nude."

"*What?*" Carol Kelleher and Pat McVeigh ask at the same time. Everybody looks at Eileen.

"I've heard too many stories about the ones with boobs out to here, or the ones drooping to the floor," Eileen says. "These poor women had to run out onto the street because they were sleeping nude when the fire broke out."

"She sleeps in an overcoat," husband Tommy says.

"With a little suitcase next to the bed. I'm going to be ready."

The jokes about beauty sleep, all the free time firefighters have, and how some call the job "white welfare" stem from how different it is from the 1960s and '70s, when 400,000 alarms were pulled in the city in a single year. New York was facing bankruptcy at the same time those partners—drugs and poverty—were tightening their grip on the city's throat. Arson was a widespread entrepreneurial endeavor. Firefighters had more than fire to fear. They became targets of inner-city anger.

In Dennis Smith's classic, *Report from Engine Co. 82*[1], he tells of getting hit in the eye with a rock while riding the side step of the fire truck; another firefighter was struck in the chest by a thrown brick. One would have been killed had he been standing a couple of feet the other way when a full garbage can hurled from the roof and slammed into the street. Firefighters were cursed at and spit on . . . the whole time being overworked and underpaid.

With the city on a one-way street towards lawlessness, it seemed the only way things would reverse themselves was if there were nothing left to burn. It took years, but from the despair and ruin rose proof of something: there's no quit in this city and certainly no quit in the FDNY.

Vigorous efforts were made to educate the public about fire safety, fire marshals aggressively investigated arson, building codes were enforced, and the city's economy started to improve. Today, fire companies have to respond to about half the number of alarms they did 25 years ago.

"It's still too dangerous," Pat says, clasping her hands.

"C'mon, my grandfather was a firefighter. He lived to 101," McVeigh says. Everybody's eyebrows are raised the way they do when an astonishing tidbit is delivered.

Tommy Carroll says with a smile, "Did he die on the job?" It's a good line, but it's not as outlandish as it seems. A lot of firefighters retire, get bored with civilian life, and sign on again. Plenty of guys want something simple said at their funeral. He died doing what he loved to do.

---

[1] Smith, Dennis. *Report From Engine Co. 82*. New York: Warner Books, 1972.

Sean Carroll, six years old, hangs on his father's neck. Brianne, Tommy's daughter, says she's bored. Tommy grabs her nose and pulls her close for a hug. He whispers that they'll be leaving in a couple of minutes.

"You doing 24?" McVeigh asks Tommy. Firefighters often work 24-hour shifts followed by a few days off.

"Nah, nine to six. Then I'm off until Wednesday, unless I pay back a tour I owe." Tommy snaps his fingers and looks at McVeigh and Kelleher. "Giants, baby. Season opener. September 10th. Monday night. You wanna catch the game at the Harbor Light?" They give noncommittal shrugs not good enough for Tommy. "I know, I know. Golf is all you care about."

"Why not? I'm retiring," McVeigh says.

Tommy leans his bottle of Coors Light to tap McVeigh's bottle. "Congrats."

McVeigh nods. "The FDNY. That's a young man's game."

■ One hundred and fifty years later, third- and fourth-generation Irish Americans still boast proudly that their recent ancestors overcame humiliating, systemic discrimination to gain a toehold of the American Dream. Don't forget that it wasn't that long ago, they'll say. The signs hung in nearly every store in New York, Boston, and other cities: No Irish Need Apply (NINA)[2].

Scholars have convincingly argued in recent years that, although such signs may have existed in London in the 1820s—mostly in the windows of private homes seeking maids—there is no evidence that such signs were posted at commercial sites in the United States. It seems that when the new Irish immigrants experienced the vagaries of the New World economy, some insisted it was due to lingering anti-Irish sentiment first cultivated in England.

Some discouraged workers started to "see" NINA signs and passed the word to others; times were tough because of prejudice.

[2] Richard Jensen, Professor, University of Illinois–Chicago. "No Irish Need Apply: A Myth of Victimization." June 2001. Available online: http://www.uic.edu/~rjensen/no-irish.htm

It was easy to personalize and accept it as fact when the country fell into economic depressions as it did in the years 1837, 1857, 1873, and 1893. However, it's difficult to refute what actually happened in other years. Businessmen who vigorously raised money for mills, factories, and construction projects knew they would employ mostly Irishmen. Irish laborers built railroads, canals, the Brooklyn Bridge, and entire city blocks.

To be sure, anti-Catholic and anti-Irish prejudice existed. The Irish came on "coffin ships" full of those who died of hunger or disease on the trip across the Atlantic. Those who survived were dirt poor and forced to live in wretched tenements. They took what jobs they could. They became street cleaners, stable hands, and porters—lowly jobs with social stigma. Their willingness to start at the bottom triggered disdain and prejudice in certain quarters. Certainly, the prejudice lingered. Al Smith's presidential candidacy in 1928 was torpedoed by such bias; parts of the South voted republican for the first time since Reconstruction. Some U.S. senators worried aloud about Smith's possible ties to the Pope. But NINA signs everywhere? It seems a contradiction when the evidence is clear that a good part of America was built on the strong backs of employed Irish.

True or not, legends of systematic, widespread prejudice grow easily in ghettos and enclaves. If there's anti-Irish sentiment out there, you'd best develop that chip on your shoulder and stick together. You go to places like Rockaway to your own kind where you're always welcome, and hear about the good jobs on the police and fire departments. You take those civil service exams that are given in English, and grab those jobs that come with a steady pay check.

Many immigrants look at civil service jobs as a rung on the ladder on the way up to the top of American society . . . wherever that is. A lot of Irish figured this was the top rung and you couldn't go higher. You shrug at the pay that could be better because you have a job you absolutely love. There are worse things than being paid to save people. If there's any more career climbing, it's to be done in the department.

Remnants of this sentiment are seen in Rockaway today. Guys like Pete Hayden and John Moran just keep going up—first on ladders, then on the chain of command: firefighter, lieutenant, captain, battalion chief, deputy chief, chief of operations, and chief of department. Some become commissioner of the entire fire department, though some don't want that job because they consider it to be more about politics than firefighting. Sometimes on the way up, they find time for more. They reach outside the FDNY and earn law degrees, as Moran did from Fordham University. When the calendar marked a new century, Hayden was deputy chief—one of the highest ranks in the department—and Moran was a battalion chief.

In the early 1970s, the starting salary for a firefighter was $11,000 a year. Now, the starting salary of a New York City firefighter is roughly $30,000; after five years, they make $50,000. The best they'll do as a regular firefighter is about $65,000, and that's with regular overtime through the year. The overtime helps, but most firefighters have second jobs with somewhat flexible work hours like bartending, nursing, construction, and painting. They have to make the extra money if they want to live in the five boroughs or anywhere close, particularly if they've got kids, as many do. Many aim to become lieutenants and captains for the better pay, not so much for the prestige and responsibilities that come with the higher rank.

In the early 1980s, a group of women successfully sued the FDNY over the physical part of the entry exam. Although the new test was still difficult, a handful of women was able to score high enough to join the Brotherhood, as some firefighters call the job. Two decades later, it's still just a handful. Of the roughly 11,000 regular firefighters in the FDNY, fewer than 30 are women. Diversity campaigns, legal challenges, and job descriptions might one day effect a change, but the FDNY is overwhelmingly male, mostly white, and largely Catholic.

Probies—firefighters fresh out of the academy—are assigned to either a ladder or engine company. It's a luck-of-the-draw kind of assignment, though it's possible to get steered one way or the other because of somebody's father or uncle.

"Hook and ladder" is a term you don't hear much anymore, but it does explain what one of the trucks brings to a fire. Ladder companies speed to fires, carrying ladders and tools such as hooks, which firefighters use to tear down ceilings or walls that might be on fire or concealing one. They also carry forcible entry tools—axes, power saws, sledge hammers, and a special pry bar called a Halligan—that will help them get into a building and ventilate it to let the smoke out. "Hook" is no longer used as a catch-all phrase and "ladder" companies are usually called "truck" companies.

In simple terms, the engine companies are the ones that put wet stuff on the red stuff. They are responsible for putting out the fire and fighting the red devil. They come with the hoses and pumps that take water from a hydrant or other source directly to the flames. The pumps boost the water pressure and force it through the hoses. Engine companies hold the nozzle. Some think it's the best job—the power position. The ceiling needs to be wet, and the guy with the nozzle points it upward. There's a flare-up in the corner, and the nozzle guy is quick to aim and douse. He's the maestro with the hose. He's in charge of the H_2O—the stuff that can whip fire. Naturally, a lot of guys love holding the nozzle.

However, there's more to it than phallic machismo. There's a simple, underlying sentiment: they know that the sooner they put out the fire, the safer everyone—including their firefighter brothers—will be.

Effective nozzle work is literally the end result of getting it right at the hydrant. Exerting and maintaining correct water pressure from the hydrant to the hose lines is essential. Four hose lines can be fed from one hydrant. A firefighter has to charge each line, then monitor the pressure on each one, making certain the pressure is adequately distributed. Too much pressure can result in the nozzle flying upward, like a bucking bronco. Being stationed off the nozzle on mid-hose, gripping a line, and feeling the water rush through can be an intimidating experience as well. You get the feeling the hose could wrap around you like a python and squeeze the life out of you, or at least leave you with some shattered bones. If they let go of the nozzle, the water or the hose itself might shoot back and knock you flat on your ass.

Nozzle work takes some muscle and usually more than a couple of hands. There is the nozzle guy in front; right behind, holding the line steady, is the backup man. Some say if one person can handle the nozzle, there's not enough pressure.

Many engines also have a small-diameter hose called a booster line, which is wound on a reel. The booster line is mainly used to put out small outdoor fires. Engines used for fighting grass or brush fires carry a tank of water and tools such as shovels and rakes. If a call comes in about an abandoned car on fire, a whole firehouse probably won't respond, but the engine will. The ladder company will stay behind.

Although nozzle work is the be-all and end-all for some, plenty of others seek ladder company work. These are the guys who charge in: they knock down doors, climb through windows, and do dangerous roof work. They're usually the ones seen "making a grab" or carrying out a terrified kid.

Each of the five boroughs of New York City has a Rescue company. Certain "odd jobs" occur that require specialized tools and equipment—SCUBA (self-contained underwater breathing apparatus) gear, hydraulic jacks, and blow torches—and training. Building collapses, subway accidents, and workers trapped in sewers or elevator shafts are all examples of incidents that sometimes require Rescue companies.

Quite often, these jobs attract the media, so if firefighter stars are born, they often come from the Rescue companies. Before getting assigned to Rescue, firefighters usually have to earn medals and show mettle. Once there, that stuff doesn't mean a thing. Now, they'd better show the established guys they're up to the job.

Straight out of the academy, firefighters are randomly assigned to engines or trucks. Eventually, they can wangle their way into the jobs they prefer.

■ A dozen kids play a sloppy touch football game in the grass lot. Across the street, the schoolyard is full of kids. In one corner, some play stickball. The outfielders are always a threat to interrupt a half-court basketball game being played on one of the eight hoops placed throughout the schoolyard. Bikes lean on the cyclone fence or are tossed on the ground—none of them with locks. Seventh graders Alex Dunn and Danny Edwards argue over a foul call. Brian Boyle hits a tennis ball over the fence into a neighbor's backyard. Joe Tyne pulls a baseball hat off of Ryan Atwood and starts running. Ryan pauses for a second, then takes off after him.

Charlie Heeran crosses Rockaway Beach Boulevard at Beach 128th Street and can see into the schoolyard. Some hoop wars, some serious basketball, has been played here over the years. You'd play all morning and then hit the beach. Hoops, beach, friends. Rockapulco. No reason to have regrets about turning down that promotion that would have sent him to London. Next summer, he might have to recruit a couple of big guys, take a shot at winning the Men's Open.

There was Mr. Lawler, his buddy Christopher's dad. On a court near The Shack—the refreshment stand that is open during summer league games—Tom Lawler holds a basketball in his hands as he speaks to his daughters, Katelyn and Jen. Mr. Lawler is giving them tips and drilling them to get ready for the upcoming season at Bishop Kearney High School in Brooklyn. He had coached them as Catholic Youth Organization (CYO) grade-school players and it was paying off in high school. Katelyn, a senior, had a chance to be All-League. Jennifer's time would come; she was just a sophomore.

Charlie doesn't want to interrupt, so he stays on the boulevard. He waves hello to Monsignor Geraghty, who is standing in front of St. Francis de Sales Church and speaking to a couple of elderly women. The guys at work told Charlie he'd better start working on his golf game if he ever wanted to make serious money. He looks again at the Monsignor. Bless me, Father, for I have sinned. I suck at golf. Charlie smiles to himself; Geraghty could absolve him of his sins and give him a few pointers. He had read in *The Wave* that the Monsignor scored a hole-in-one last year.

He turns on the next corner (Beach 130th Street), nodding hello to people he knows, waving to Richie Allen who is heading into his mother's house. He'd have to ask Richie how he likes being a Probie. Bet he loves it. Richie is several years older and had joined the FDNY a bit later than most. He'd been with the sanitation department, been a New York City teacher, and had always been a summer lifeguard. He always helps people, so the fire department would be a good fit.

As Charlie crosses Newport Avenue, he sees George Johnson on the sidewalk heading his way. For a second, he thinks about hurrying across the street and bolting up the steps into the Harbor Light, where he would surely find somewhere to hide. His father, Bernie, retired from the FDNY for a year, owns the place, and Charlie knows every inch. He'd better know every inch because he planned on running the place himself one day.

George is after him to play rugby for the Rockaway club—the Fisheads—but so far, Charlie is keeping his promise to his dad to stay retired. Too dangerous, too easy to get hurt, but the rugby guys won't let up. Charlie is good, and both Rockaway and the Manhattan Rugby Club are coaxing him to play.

"Hey, you're one of the Rockaway Irish Boys, ain't you?" George asks.

Charlie steps from the street and takes a quick glance at the green awning above the door to the Harbor Light. He can still make a run for it. "Hey, George," Charlie says, smiling, knowing George's question was a guilt-soaked recruiting pitch.

Anywhere from 50 to 150 sand-in-their-shoes blood brothers call themselves the RIBs (Rockaway Irish Boys) to stamp the deep kinship they built growing up on the beach. Each of the guys would have six or seven "best" friends. One might say of another, "He's like my best, best friend," but most times "best" meant one of several. Once a year, at least 60 or so throw themselves a party at the Harbor Light. Younger guys like Charlie and Chris sometimes call themselves the Baby Backs. The guys, a couple of years older, call themselves the Prime Ribs. A humorist for *The Wave* noted their neighborhood social presence with a wink: "The Rockaway Irish Boys (RIBs) are now reviewing applications for fall membership. Among the stringent requirements are a healthy alcohol tolerance, passing grade on the firefighter's written test, an inherent distrust of all things female, and your own apartment (or at least parents who travel frequently)."

Charlie is a Rockaway boy, for sure. He could've moved into Manhattan, but an apartment on Beach 108th Street is just fine. Still, he is hearing it from guys at work like Matt Burke, who had played rugby for Xavier High School just like Charlie had. They'd say he could live wherever he wanted, but he should play rugby for the Manhattan club.

He would resist Manhattan, George knew that. He just wanted to get him thinking about playing. George is a firefighter, the son of a firefighter, and a brother to two firefighters. It's deep in his bones. He still remembers the smoky smell of his father's gear in the back of an old Volkswagen Beetle. Sometimes his father would take him along to the firehouse when he was picking up his pay check. What a treat. It was great as a wide-eyed little boy and it was great now—11 years after signing on himself.

That's not to say there isn't room in his heart for another passion. A good chunk of his ticker is reserved for rugby. An FDNY shield rests on the dashboard of his car, but on the rear bumper is a sticker: "Give Blood Play Rockaway Rugby."

"It's one thing to pick finance over fire, but you're a Rockaway boy. You can't be playing for Manhattan," George says.

Bernie Heeran comes from around the side of the building, spraying the sidewalk with a garden hose. "You miss the fire department that much, Bernie?" George says, looking at the hose, then back at Bernie.

"Yeah, funny," he says, blasting a couple of cigarette butts into the gutter. Bernie can be gruff, but he's ripped up a lot of bills, often refusing to take payment after groups have come in for a meal after a funeral. He's got season tickets for St. John's University basketball, but he usually hands them to parents of kids who seem to like the game. He's used basketball connections to help local kids get into colleges where they can eke out a few more years of competitive ball. "Leave him alone," Bernie adds. "He's gotta slow down. He's got too much going on and he's staying on Wall Street."

"Rugby. I'm talking about rugby," George says, throwing his arm around Charlie and giving him a one-armed bear hug.

Bernie has reasons to want to keep his sons on Wall Street. Just a few years back, on St. Patrick's night, while working the nozzle on a good job, he was inadvertently pushed from behind, his head slammed on a metal doorframe, and was knocked unconscious. When you have to call "Mayday" and get your lungs scorched, you get a new perspective on the job.

If he ever needed a reminder about how tough things could be, he just had to remember the families from Worcester, Massachusetts. Some time after his close call, he'd been working in the marine division of the FDNY and had given a New York tour to the families of firefighters who had died in a Worcester warehouse fire. Meeting the kids was heartbreaking stuff. Then he joined the HELP team at Kings County Hospital. HELP is a group of light-duty firefighters who visit injured firefighters to keep them company and make certain their needs are being met. It's selfless and rewarding work, and gives yet another view about how dangerous the job can be. No, he doesn't want Charlie or his other sons Billy and Sean having anything to do with fire.

"We're playing in Jersey tomorrow. What do you say, Charlie?" George says.

"The way he can see the court, he should still be playing basketball." Bernie shoots the hose towards their feet, making them dance like cowpokes in a TV western. They both run up the steps into the Harbor Light.

■ It's the neighborhood place. Once a seasonal lodge, it's a three-story frame building with Cape Cod gray shingles. A dining room set in dark timber sits off the bar. Seafood, steaks, and fat, juicy burgers keep the place busy just about every night of the week.

Upstairs, there's a room for communion parties and bridal show-ers. Bernie rents the top floor apartment to the chef's brother, who happens to be a firefighter.

The bar is dark and smoky. If your eyes can adjust to the dark and the smoke, you'll see walls lined with yellowed pictures of sports heroes and laminated news accounts of local athletes. A couple of TVs above the bar are wedged into the corners of the room. A jukebox leans against a post, lonely and silent most times. A third TV—a 50-inch monster—sits in a corner, ignored unless a really big game is on.

Bernie Heeran—mid-'50s, silver haired with sharp, blue eyes—has run the Harbor Light for more than 20 years. He and his fire-fighter buddy, Wally Hynes, bought it when it was called Pete's Place; before that, it was the Newport Inn. They saved some money by doing a lot of the kitchen work themselves, which they were prepared to do having honed considerable culinary talents at the firehouse. They hired firefighters and family to bartend and wait tables. Customers were firefighters as well, but it never became strictly a firefighter's place. Bernie is a basketball coach, too, so he makes sure sports fans and jocks feel at home. He also has a nice touch with families who arrive for lunch after a funeral mass held at St. Francis, just down the block.

It has earned local landmark status because it's the stepping-off point for the annual Rockaway St. Patrick's Day Parade, usually held on a Saturday before the grand New York version. It's a big enough deal that New York's mayor and any politician who wants a vote from Rockaway show up. Of course, the real fun doesn't start until about the same time the politicians are in their cars leaving Rockaway. That's when a mass of people meets under a tent set up in the parking lot of the Harbor Light. Families of three and four generations toast and hoist until the sun goes down. Kids, usually away at college, come home that weekend with col-lege pals to give them a taste of what many call the wildest day of the year in Rockaway.

You'll hear plenty of festive bagpipes and Clancy Brothers and U2. Chances are you'll hear a crowd burst into a chorus of *Ooh ah up the Ra, say ooh ah up the Ra* from "Celtic Symphony" by the Wolfe Tones—the unofficial anthem of Rockaway youth. Of course, by the end of the night, old-timers will know the rest of the song, too. With their sons and daughters, they'll be singing *Graffiti on the walls that says We're Magic! We're Magic!* You'll certainly meet some of the RIBs, and maybe they'll be belting out Paddy Reilly's "The Town I Loved So Well" or something a tad more boisterous like "Hells Bells" by AC/DC.

On other, more sober, nights, the Harbor Light is full of people who know your name but also know your Achilles heel. If you can laugh at yourself, you'll feel at home. Tommy Carroll tells the story of the time he got his picture in the *Daily News* for helping carry out a kid from a burning building in Brooklyn. Hero for the day, he went to the Harbor Light, figuring he wouldn't have to buy a drink. He'd start his diet the next day. As soon as he walked in, he heard, "I saw your picture in the paper. Jeez, you got more chins than a Chinese phone book." He took a few more comments about showing off, and then everybody at the bar gave him a round of applause.

You might get a similar reaction if your kid won a scholarship or you just coached a local team to a championship. Sure, some guys in the Harbor Light look like they were born on a hook and ladder, but they could be stockbrokers or lawyers. The Belle Harbor neighborhood in Rockaway is an even mix of blue- and white-collar workers, and you can't see either color in the cheerful dimness of the Harbor Light.

Bernie hoses the sidewalk, then spritzes the flower bed in front. Early September can be a little slow, but he's expecting a good crowd for Monday night football—the Giants' first league game since Super Bowl IX months earlier. John Moran toots his horn as he drives past.

Around the corner, Tommy Carroll comes out of Curran's, the local butcher shop, and bumps into Danny Suhr. The two could be mammoth bookends, if anything could squeeze between them. Fair-haired and brawny, forearm slabs, the two were teammates on the Brooklyn Mariners, a legendary football team coached by

Pudgie Walsh—himself a legend and a firefighter once profiled in *Sports Illustrated*. They both suited up for the fire department's football team a few years back. Tommy asks if he'll be going to the Harbor Light to catch the Giants' game. Danny says he can't because of too much work to do on his house, and the fact that he's got to do a 24 in the morning.

Tommy tries coaxing him. "Watch the first half."

Danny's not budging. "Hey, I need to get my floors sanded." He says it, knowing Tommy will have a name for him.

"Call Kevin Dowdell," Tommy suggests, referring to a Breezy Point firefighter.

"From Rescue 4? He does floors?"

"Yep, and there's your painter." Tommy points at Brian Becker—another firefighter—heading into the 29 Deli. "Work the firefighter phone book," he says, as McVeigh pulls into the parking spot at the curb. "Look at this. If you ever wanna move, here's your moving man. He'll have the time . . . he's retiring." Standing in front of Jameson's, a pub just a few stores down, was Chucky Kavanaugh. "If you want to go drinking, there's your man."

"When these guys want a pizza, they call me," Danny says.

"That's what I tell 'em."

Danny owns a pizza place in Brooklyn. He says he'll be going straight to the store after he gets off from the firehouse on Wednesday morning. "You'll get me Dowdell's number?"

"I'll call you at the firehouse tomorrow. You at 216?"

Suhr nods yes and then starts up the block. Tommy calls after him, "I hope you got Timmy Reid to do your electric."

■ A groan rolls out the door and onto the street just as Pete Hayden ties Guinness, his golden retriever, to an awning post in front of the Harbor Light. It can't be good news for the Giants if the fans inside the place are groaning this loudly and this early in the game. Hayden is stopping by to watch a little of the game, but mostly to say hello to his brother, Jack, who is tending bar.

Hayden walks into the crowded bar and is hit with the kind of cigarette and cigar smoke that makes him wish he had a mask. He says hello to Bernie Heeran and shakes hands with old friends. He sees too many firefighters to count. Most of them live nearby, close enough to walk home. Some stand with wives or girlfriends at chest-high tables; others stand in clusters at the bar.

Look at these guys, Hayden thinks to himself. They don't get enough of each other on the job, they have to watch football together, too. He tries to remember their names when they say, "Hello, Chief," though plenty of them know him long enough to say, "What's up, Pete?" Even though he is way up in the fire department, he is still a regular guy.

He'd done a good 15 years of what his brother is doing right now—working a second job behind the bar at the Harbor Light. It had helped put five kids through school. Time was flying; he was pulling draft beers when it was called the Newport Inn. Thirty-four years on the FDNY makes time shoot by.

Let's see: there's Palmer Doyle, Tommy Carroll, Kevin Judge, the Collins brothers, Eddie Greene, Kevin Lunny, Matt Tansey, Harry Werner, Billy Gallagher and Farmer. Then there were easy ones: guys he knew forever, like Pete Brady and Johnny Mac-Namara. There's Mike Moran, John's brother. Jeez, New York could burn down tonight! Wasn't anybody working? Even brother Jack, behind the bar, is a firefighter. At least the Harbor Light is safe, even if you needed a Halligan tool to cut the smoke. Five or six college-age kids look past their girlfriends at Hayden. A couple of them have the look: the flunking-out-of-school-doesn't-matter look. They want to be firefighters.

A roar suddenly erupts. Giants' quarterback Kerry Collins hits Amani Toomer for a tying touchdown. Life is good. All is right with the world again.

Charlie Heeran weaves through the crowd with an armful of beers, giving away one after another until he's got one left to hand to Chris Lawler. "What'd you buy, a case again?"

"Nah, nah. Not this time. Just a few." The week before at "Hat Night"—part of a Labor Day weekend tradition when some locals wear funny and outrageous hats—Charlie made the bartender do a double-take when he ordered 24 bottles of beer at the rugby clubhouse. He had just shrugged at the time. "Hey, everybody should have a beer, if they want one."

Charlie nods at Chris, who is standing suspiciously near the jukebox. "You're not gonna play 'My Way.'"

"With the Giants' game on? I'm not *that* crazy."

Charlie smiles and taps Chris on the elbow. "Hey, we're in."

"Yeah?"

Charlie just got the okay from Bernie, his father. He and Chris can be guest bartenders on the night before Thanksgiving—the second best bar night of the year. Sometimes it's even better than St. Paddy's. They'll make hundreds in tips. It is especially good news for Chris, a second-year law student at St. John's.

"That's great, 'cause I'll be broke by then," Chris says, "and it'll be a blast."

"It's gonna be sick," Charlie says, then tugs at Chris's shirt. "Maybe we'll go Hawaiian?"

"Hawaiian shirts behind the bar at the Harbor Light? I don't think so."

Palmer Doyle tries to squeeze by, but then stops when he recognizes Charlie. "Hey, Charlie, what's happening? Where you working now?"

"Cantor Fitzgerald." It isn't hard to detect the pride in his voice. Cantor Fitzgerald is one of the biggest bond trading companies in New York.

"Yeah, yeah, yeah. One of those places where they make millionaires out of billionaires."

Charlie laughs easily and then adds, "Hey, I'm not even a thousandaire yet." He figures he'll have his first million by the time he's 30. Until then, he'll need some bartending shifts.

Palmer nods at Chris. "What about you? You still gonna be Perry Mason or Johnnie Cochran?"

Charlie and Chris laugh, then take swigs of beer. "Uh, yes, I'm still in law school," Chris says. The crowd suddenly lets go with curses and groans. Denver has gone ahead 14-7.

The bar loses a good part of the crowd at half-time. The game looks like it won't end until after midnight and just about everybody has to work tomorrow. Tommy Carroll barks good-naturedly at the fair-weather fans giving up on his team at half-time. "We're the comeback kids. You can't be walking out."

Jack Hayden, behind the stick, shrugs.

Tommy's optimism looks well founded as the Giants tie the game in the third quarter, but soon he's pulling on his wind-breaker, too. The game gets ugly in a hurry. Denver goes out in front, 31-14. He stops to chat with an old-timer, Mike Sullivan. They talk about firefighters they both know, like Pudgie Walsh and Richie O'Grady. Sullivan says he hears Joe Angelini is still working. "He must be 63, 64 years old. How do you stay on?"

In the 1970s, when fire companies couldn't keep up with all the fires, a lot of men had premonitions. They fought so many fires that a lot of them started to figure it was only a matter of time before fate would see to it that a ceiling would fall on them or a floor would collapse underneath them. Sullivan said he started getting gun shy. "There were just too many fires. Sooner or later . . ." He lets the thought drift as he crushes a cigarette into an ash-tray. "You guys don't got the same worries today, and that's good."

Tommy can't argue. He really doesn't worry too much about getting hurt or killed. He watches the final seconds tick away, the Giants falling 31-20.

"Eight, 10 guys a year used to die," Sullivan says, still looking back.

Tommy shakes his head. Eight or 10? No thanks. The department is still reeling from the Father's Day fire a couple of months ago, when three men were killed in a fire in Astoria.

Credits are rolling on the TV screen. Tommy glances at Sullivan's wristwatch. "Jesus, it's already Tuesday."

CHAPTER 2

Like Any Other Morning

September 1892

Rockaway—a splinter of land surrounded by water—has had its history carved by fire. In the early part of the 19th century, accessible only by private yacht or by stagecoach on a turnpike paved with seashells through private Long Island towns, Rockaway drew New York aristocrats. The Marine Pavilion, with Doric peristyles and a piazza 235 feet long and 20 feet wide, stood boastfully at the spectacular oceanfront while accommodating guests such as Washington Irving, Henry Wadsworth Longfellow, and various Astors and Vanderbilts. It is said that ocean swimming and bathing came into style with the opening of the Marine Pavilion in 1833. The hotel became known throughout the United States, and soon other large, fashionable hotels were built in Rockaway.

In 1864, fire made the Marine Pavilion a memory. It would still be a few more years before Rockaway had its first volunteer fire department. Extinguishing the blaze was impossible; stopping it from spreading was the only hope. While the fire raged, men dynamited nearby structures to keep the fire contained.

The introduction of railroads and ferries in the latter half of the century made the peninsula far less stylish. The upper crust retreated eastward to the Hamptons, while the lower middle class invaded Rockaway, giving the peninsula decidedly Jewish and Irish flavors.

The Irish came to Rockaway as owners and tenants, businessmen and customers—some to live and some for an afternoon of fresh ocean air. Hotels, bungalows, and tent colonies sprung up along with arcades and other amusements in communities called Seaside, Irish Town, and Arverne.

Men named Murphy, Callaghan, Burke, and O'Kelly stocked 10 volunteer fire departments throughout the growing resort. Horses pulled some steam-operated pumping engines, but most of the equipment was heaped and lugged on hand-drawn carriages. All this proved inadequate in the great Seaside fire of 1892.

On Tuesday, September 13, volunteer firefighters—vollies—from Beach 90th Street rushed to the Seaside Hotel on Beach 103rd Street to put out the flames; hours later, it was left in ashes. A week later, the ruins reignited. Before the vollies from fire companies called Seaside Hose and Oceanus Ladder arrived, a conflagration was underway. Hotels, restaurants, the Seaside museum, Kingsland's Casino, Garrison's Bakery, and Mary Boyle's Boarding House were wrapped in flames, as overmatched firefighters tried to contain the blaze. They summoned all fire companies within 4 miles of Rockaway, but knew that even extra troops meant little to the fire being stoked by its accomplice: the 30-mile-per-hour wind coming off the ocean. Heated by the fire, the wind acted like a blowtorch, preheating everything in its path that wasn't already ablaze. Embers propelled by the fierce wind caused spot fires at buildings blocks apart, which thinned the firefighting ranks and exhausted the meager water supply.

As word got out, hundreds of firefighters from Brooklyn and Queens arrived on trains, but their willingness to battle was thwarted—there was simply not enough water. There were no water mains to supply water, and the lone water tower quickly ran dry. What little water they got came from wells (holes 800 feet deep in the ground). Because the water pressure was so weak, firefighters had to stand on the fire itself to get water on the blaze. One witness said it was like being lost at sea and dying of thirst. All that ocean and bay water, good for nothing.

The fast fire burned for seven hours until there was nothing left to consume. Four blocks—from the Atlantic Ocean to Jamaica Bay—were completely incinerated. Nineteen hotels, numerous arcades, restaurants, and small businesses were simply gone. A once-bustling center of amusement was now a stretch of black, flattened rubble. Although residents

could see the devastation and smell the smoke for days, they felt enormous relief: just one person died and the number of injured was small. At
the time, Rockawayites usually got their news from the Brooklyn
Eagle. With the delivery of the paper delayed because trains were being
used to move firefighters and apparatus, a local printer named James
Keenan put out a newsletter providing locals with as much information
as he could gather. The untitled newsletter carried a headline: "Wave of
Fire Strikes Rockaway."

The newsletter grew into a newspaper, with that first headline serving
as inspiration for the paper's permanent name, The Wave—now New
York's oldest weekly newspaper. It's a nearly forgotten anecdote; residents think the paper is named for the community's proximity to the
Atlantic Ocean.

The Rockaway Seaside fire happened in the fall of 1892. Just a few
months later, the United States fell into economic depression. Rockaway
people hardly noticed. They began rebuilding as soon as the ashes cooled.

September 2001

Tommy Carroll turns off his car radio as soon as he hears the
announcer say something about the "sports recap in a minute."
He doesn't want to be reminded that his Giants lost the night
before—shit, just seven hours before. He figures they'd beat Kan-
sas City next weekend. Come home 1-1 for the Home Opener.

He still isn't used to the back-to-school schedule. It isn't easy in
the summer, but figuring out where the kids are going to be in
September always seems like a major hassle. Each week, he and
Eileen would have to figure out a schedule about picking up the
kids from school. If neither could be home in mid-afternoon,
they'd get either a friend or a baby-sitter.

He taps the steering wheel at a red light on Flatbush Avenue,
trying to get things straight in his head. He glances at the digital
clock on the dashboard. Eileen was on her way to work—a good
three-times-a week job at Paine Webber in mid-town. She
wouldn't be home until after 7 PM, which meant he'd be home
first. He would have to zip home—no bullshitting after work—to

relieve the baby-sitter. You couldn't overburden the baby-sitter so early in the school year or else you might lose her.

Next year, T.J. would be in high school—one less to worry about. He'd only be a tuition worry at that point, especially if he got into Xavier High School. However, with Brianne in sixth grade and Sean just in first, Tommy knew he'd better accept schedule-juggling as a fact of life.

If he could only get it straight whether or not Sean was going to play fall soccer, which might involve an afternoon and Saturday mornings. Brianne would be on the swim team. They had practice at least one night a week in Brooklyn or Long Beach, and swim meets on Sundays. He'd have to give Brian and Barbara King a call about taking turns driving. T.J. was already practicing a couple of nights a week with his football team in Broad Channel. He was good about arranging rides for himself. Now if the kid would only put on some weight. He loves to play but he's got Eileen's build.

Tommy arrives at his Brooklyn firehouse on Dean Street a few minutes before 8 AM, feeling like he shouldn't even be there. He owes the city a tour—the result of a "self-mutual" he had taken weeks before. When he sought to pay it back yesterday (Monday), a cranky chief nixed his request.

■ New York City firefighters have flexible work schedules built around nine- and 15-hour work shifts. The nine-hour shift is fairly standard: 9 AM to 6 PM. The 15-hour shift runs from 6 PM until 9 AM the next morning. When firefighters say they're doing a "24," it means they'll be on duty for 24 straight hours, working the nine- and 15-hour shifts back to back. Sometimes they're kept busy through the 24 hours; other times, they're able to get several hours of sleep in the bunks at the firehouse, though it's often not the most restful sleep.

Somewhat like doctors in their residency who grab sleep when they can, firefighters never know if they'll get a long stretch of sleep or be summoned to duty at any time. Light sleepers are at the mercy of heavy snorers. If there's a reward in working a 24, it's not about the chance to sleep—it's the next 2-1/2 days (or more) off.

A firefighter can ask a buddy to work for him with the understanding he'll pay it back. That's a "mutual"—you work for me, I'll work for you when you need it. It's a good way to clear time for a second job or short vacation; however, the modest pay check from the city tends to limit vacations. So, if a firefighter works a 24, gets a couple of days off, and nabs a mutual followed by the usual few days off, he's managed to carve out a week "off" without using vacation or sick time.

The FDNY allows for "self-mutuals" as well. Instead of asking a buddy or another firefighter to complete the mutual, a firefighter can ask for a mutual through official channels, in which case the department finds the replacement. When done this way, the firefighter "owes" the FDNY—or the city—a tour. The opposite is also an option. On days they're scheduled to be off, they can make themselves available for work. Doing this, firefighters can "bank" up to two tours, knowing they'll need the time off at some point.

▪ Tommy owes the city a tour and wants to get it out of the way. Most of the time, it's done without a hitch. He would call in and say he wanted to pay back a tour. A chief's aide would tell him, "No problem," or, in this case, "It looks good, but call back and confirm."

On the confirmation call Sunday evening, he got the chief himself and the guy's a simple crank. "No, you can't work Monday. We don't need you."

Great. He owes the tour and this guy's telling him he can't work, which puts him in a bind. If he doesn't settle up, they won't allow him to do mutuals. He's got to pay it back. Late Sunday night, he finally found a more agreeable chief who said it was too late to work Monday but to come in on Tuesday, September 11.

Tommy had wanted Tuesday off because the weather was supposed to be nice. That meant construction work, which is dependent on the weather, would be available. In a perfect world, he would've paid back the city on Monday and, right now, on this gorgeous Tuesday morning, he'd be halfway through a day of bending steel.

No such luck.

When you owe a tour, you're likely to be "detailed" to another fire company to satisfy a manpower shortage. Even if you're in for regular duty, you might still be detailed. Sometimes this means going across the floor. More than half the firehouses in New York are "double houses," meaning they have an engine and a truck (ladder) company. If a firefighter is normally assigned to the engine but the truck is short on personnel, he or she can be detailed within the same firehouse—or, in other words, "across the floor."

Detail assignments are somewhat a matter of personal preference. Some firefighters don't mind getting detailed because they like an occasional change of scenery; some gladly accept details because it might mean they'll be closer to home or closer to their second job. Some do it for the extra $40—the bonus the FDNY pays to firefighters accepting the detail. If you get detailed across the floor, you don't get the extra money.

It can take a while to get a handle on mutuals and the details of details. It's an art as much as a code. There's a "book," of course, with rules and regulations, but there's also the "unwritten book," which, for most guys, works better. If there is the need to detail more than one firefighter, the senior man gets first dibs. Firefighters with 20 years or more on the job—affectionately called "golden cows" by some—don't have to accept any detail.

For all their quirkiness, mutuals and details are considerable perks, and firefighters make sure their union reps know they're not to be bargained away. They are perks, to be sure, but they've long figured into the puzzle of fate. You take a detail and it saves your life, or you don't take a detail and it gets you killed. You might be paying back a mutual at the right time or for the last time.

The shift starts at 9 AM, but most firefighters show up at least a half hour early to relieve the guy on duty and let him head home early. Plenty of times, however, the firefighter getting relieved hangs around, in no real hurry to go anywhere, unless he's got to get to a second job.

The Dean Street firehouse is a "double house"—one with an engine company, with the hoses, and a ladder or truck. More than half of the approximately 220 firehouses in the five boroughs are double houses. Single houses—one engine or one truck—are usually a matter of real estate. An engine and a truck will cover a common area, but they won't necessarily be housed together because there might not be an appropriately sized building available.

Although subject to negotiations between the city, the union, and the FDNY brass, engine companies routinely consist of six people (five firefighters and an officer, a lieutenant or a captain). Many firefighters grumble when the city insists on "five men on a six-man job." One of the firefighters, called the chauffeur, drives the engine; sitting next to him is the officer. Four firefighters ride on the "back step," although, in a strict sense, they no longer do.

For decades, firefighters used to jump and stand on the back step of the engine or truck seconds before it pulled out of the garage on the way to a fire. They would stand in open air for the ride—hanging on to bars, straps, or equipment as the apparatus raced to a fire. Too many men got hurt falling off on fast, sharp turns or by sudden stops. Though firefighters now sit inside, they still call it the back step. During a shift in a single house, those six will be the only personnel in the firehouse. Likewise, the ladder or truck company will have five firefighters and an officer. In double houses, there will be as many as 12 people working during a shift (10 firefighters and two officers).

■ Tommy is not crazy about working this morning, but he's happy to see Captain Timmy Stackpole when he first enters the firehouse. He has known Stackpole since they played Pee-Wee football together.

"Hey, look at you. This your first day?" he says to Stackpole.

"Second."

"Oh, you got it down already."

Stackpole's got a big smile. He was promoted to captain just a few days before. He had made the rank against many odds. Three years earlier, more than 30% of his body was burned after a floor collapsed at a fire in East New York. He could have retired with a comfortable pension, but instead came back to the job and life he loved. Now he was captain. Because he was a new captain, he'd do what new ones do: bounce from house to house for months until a permanent spot opened, usually when someone retired. His first two-day tours were at Engine 219.

"When you movin' to Rockaway?" Tommy asks.

"I'm lookin', but I can't do it. Not yet."

"You got five kids. That's a Rockaway family," Tommy says.

"I know, I know, but I gotta wait, I think."

Tommy nods; he understands. While he was recovering in a burn unit, off-duty firefighter friends renovated Stackpole's house in Marine Park, Brooklyn—just across the water from Rockaway. They'd begun the work as a surprise gift.

"My mother-in-law lives in Rockaway, so we're halfway there."

Firefighter Henry Miller and Captain Vinny Brunton of Ladder 105 join in the morning chitchat near the booth at the front of the house. It's early, but not so early that Tommy can't tease his friend Frankie Palumbo who is passing by. Frankie is the father of 10 kids.

"Frankie, is Jeannie pregnant?" Tommy asks.

"No!"

"Hey, if you got problems, maybe you should try that in vitro thing."

Frank lets go with a good laugh, which is a relief to the others who are wincing, thinking Tommy had managed to malign Frankie's steadfast adherence to Catholic doctrine.

"What about *your* parents?" Frankie says.

"They were birth control freaks compared to you two!" Tommy waves a dismissive hand. Everyone gets another good laugh. Tommy is one of eight kids himself.

Stackpole, thinking his brood of five is modest around here, says he'd like to stay, but he's got to report to division headquarters because he's listed as surplus today, meaning there's no firehouse in need of an officer today. It's just past 8:30 AM when he heads out.

Henry Miller, on house watch, tells Tommy that he's got a choice of details. He can go over to Engine 226, or take the detail "across the floor" because 105 needs a body. John Chipura is facing a detail as well, but it's Tommy's call because he's the senior man of the two. Engine 226 firehouse is close—just several blocks away—and Tommy senses that John wants a change of pace from the engine and would be pleased to get on the truck.

"You sure? You're senior," John says.

"No problem. I can send my kids to college on the detail money."

John chuckles and says thanks. Tommy waves off the thanks. He's scheduled to work three straight day tours, so taking a detail to another house will be a welcome change of pace.

Firefighters catching a detail have 45 minutes to report to the assigned firehouse, which means Tommy won't be expected at Engine 226 until 9:45 AM. Because the detail is so close, Tommy is in no hurry and has more time to shoot the breeze with Brunton, Chipura, Palumbo, and Miller.

The phone rings and Miller picks it up. This time, Engine 226 is calling back, asking if the detail for their house has left already and, if not, would he mind going to 210 instead. The caller tells Miller that Engine 226 has filled its spot and now 210 could use a chauffeur. Miller knows Tommy is a chauffeur, so he glances at Tommy still standing there and says yes into the phone, figuring it won't matter to Tommy if he goes to 226 or 210. He's right; even though 210 is a bit further away, Tommy doesn't mind at all.

Tommy had resisted chauffeur school because, once you start driving the rig, you're essentially allowing others to fight fires. Chauffeurs of engines stay with the rig while others drag the hose into burning buildings. Another captain at the firehouse, Donnie Howard, had nudged him enough, reminding him that it's not a bad option to have as you pile up years on the way to a pension. After hemming and hawing and grousing for months, Tommy finally gave in and went to chauffeur school. If he hadn't made that decision, if he hadn't been pushed by Donnie Howard, he probably wouldn't be going to 210 today.

Before he pulls out in his car for the drive to the other firehouse, he's reminded that the 210 firehouse is under construction and the company is sharing quarters with Ladder 119 and Engine 211, a bit further away in the Williamsburg section of Brooklyn. It's such a nice day and Tommy doesn't mind a longer drive. Hey, he's no longer annoyed at the chief who made him work today instead of yesterday.

■ The waves are big—once-a-year big. Although it's a Tuesday morning and the summer crowds are gone, the water's filling up with college kids playing hooky, or guys with flexible work schedules like firefighters—like Whipper Stathis. He's just dropped the kids off at school and, now that he's seen the waves, he'll go home and get his board. He'll join the other firefighters in the water. He thinks he can spot Dennis Farrell and his kid, Sunny, but first he's got to swallow as much of that cleansing ocean air as he can. Nothing like it.

It's always been the best time of year in Rockaway. The beach is empty, the waves are big, and the water's still holding the summer sun. Whipper's 45, but he still feels like the kid who learned how to surf before he learned how to swim. That's why it's okay to call him Whipper, instead of his given name of Peter. Whipper is short for whippersnapper—the name some old crank called him in front of all his friends a million years ago. In Rockaway, nicknames stick like tar on your sneakers. You have middle-aged men called Turtle, Bugsy, Peg, Leaper, Chin, Flip, Farmer, Whopper, Suntan, and Captain Crunch. With all the Tommys and Kevins in the neighborhood, maybe it's easier.

To Whipper, it feels like yesterday when Rockaway kids were surfing on their mother's ironing boards, though there are plenty of reminders that yesterday has been gone a while. Kids show off on the newest short boards, and Wall Street guys and lawyers arrive on the A train carrying vintage long boards. Sunglasses cost a hundred bucks. He could do without those changes, but you can't argue about the water these days. The ocean has never been this clean. No medical waste, no sludge, no Coney Island White Fish—floating condoms that seemed as common as jellyfish. If the water's waist high, you can still see your feet. The banks of the New Jersey shore look close today, like there's been a continental land shift overnight.

Whipper wonders if Kenny Whelan, captain of the local fire-house and lifelong friend, is already in the water. Kenny and his wife, Roseanne, were on late summer vacation two hours away on Long Beach Island in New Jersey. Some people leave Rockaway for beach vacations; they want a change of scenery, but nothing too drastic. They don't want the phone to ring and they don't want to find bills in the mailbox, but they still want sand and surf, both of which look really good to Whipper right now. He's not on vacation, but he'll feel like it once he gets his board. He may as well because there's nothing else going on.

There doesn't seem to be much happening anywhere else, either. The *Daily News* is trying to stir interest in the mayoral primary; the public yawns. There's a story about Rudolph Giuliani wrapping up his stint as mayor; New Yorkers are growing tired of him as well. The sports news is about the football Giants and the Yankees. A *New York Post* story carries this headline: "Only Drama Is In Trainer's Room," referring to a couple of players with nagging injuries; Yankee fans aren't worried.

The stock market is still in a post-dot-com daze, with the Dow floundering at 10,000 after being at 11,500 several months before. The NASDAQ is half of what it was. George Bush is a president with chads hanging over his head, and a good many people wonder if he deserves to be in the Oval Office at all after he was awarded the presidency by the U.S. Supreme Court.

The Little League makes major league headlines when it's discovered that a 14-year-old with an amazing pitching arm is not 14 at all—he's actually 16 and armed with a phony birth certificate. It's another cheating scandal, which the tabloids and the public seem to love. Danny Almonte is front-page news the way Gary

Condit is, the way Bill Clinton was. Important news is gossipy, too. Colin Powell, according to *Newsweek*, is the odd man out in the Bush administration.

■ Charlie Heeran gets to work at 6:45 AM. From the 104th floor of One World Trade Center, he can see for miles. On some days, it seems that you can see Canada on one side of the building, and on the west side all the way to Ohio—though most days it's usually tough to see anything past Jersey City. Yet, the east side is often clear.

From a nearby window, Charlie can see the Marine Park Bridge (Marine Parkway Gil Hodges Memorial Bridge), which connects Brooklyn to Rockaway. It's a blur, but he figures he can guess exactly where the Harbor Light is from here: a quarter of a mile up in the air, 13 miles away, and he can still see home.

After taking in the view during the first couple of weeks at work, Charlie is now more interested in viewing the morning numbers. He doesn't have much concern about the Dow Jones and other popular indices. He works on the Institutional Equities desk. His company, Cantor Fitzgerald, serves institutional—rather than individual—customers, frequently serving as a broker between large organizations wishing to keep their trading strategies secret by dealing with each other indirectly.

At the trading desk, smiles come up with the sun. Charlie is telling stories about his frat house at the University of Scranton, and how they paid the rent one time by having "Schaefer Beer Night." He and Pete Hayden, son of the fire chief, bought cases of the dirt-cheap beer, invited a bunch of people to a party, and then charged enough at the door to make the landlord happy.

He gets a call from a buddy, Sean Fitzgerald, and there are more stories and laughs, though he has one eye on the computer screen before him. He needs to get ready for the day. The market will open soon.

■ Matt Tansey, 27, doesn't mind extending his shift. By trading tours—now he'd work until 6 PM and then have Wednesday off—

he'll be able to free a chunk of time to work on his Rockaway apartment. He'd bought the studio apartment right off the bay for next to nothing. Once he fixes it up—the floors, the kitchen—he'll have himself a nice place to live as well as a good investment. He'll always be able to rent the place if he ever bought a house. Of course, the fixing might have to wait until next week. The waves at the beach are the best of the year.

Matt and his friend, Mike Mullan, stand side by side brushing their teeth, both feeling rested after a quiet night at the firehouse on West 19th Street in Chelsea. Mullan says he's getting engaged and has to buy an engagement ring.

"Look no further," Matt tells him. "My mom is good friends with a jeweler. You won't get ripped off and they'll make sure you get something nice."

Another firefighter, Angel Juarbe, is flipping through the classifieds, looking at real estate. Over the summer, he'd been a contestant on a Fox-TV reality show, *Murder In Small Town X*, and had won first prize. He'd just gotten the check for $250,000 in the mail last week. Not enough to retire on, but enough to put a big down payment on a house somewhere.

Matt tells Angel he should check the houses in Rockaway. "You like the beach, right? Maybe get a two-family." Angel nods; that sounds nice.

Someone jokes, "Yeah, you gotta win a contest to afford Rockaway."

Matt could use a cigarette, so he goes out front on the street and joins an old Rockaway guy, Steve Belson, for a smoke. Belson (or "Bells" to friends) had a bad back and was almost forced from the job, but he fought the department doctors and said he was staying one way or the other, even if it meant chauffeuring or being a chief's aide. That was the compromise they made: he was permitted to stay, but it had to be as a driver—a safer, far less strenuous position than a regular firefighter. For Bells, it wasn't perfect, but it was better than getting out altogether.

Matt knew him from the beach. Although Bells was much older (he was 51), they both loved to surf and had taken the path common to many Rockaway guys. You spend your teens as a lifeguard and then join the fire department as soon as you can. They both talked about the big surf crushing the sand with that hurricane off Bermuda. Matt got a kick out of Steve—especially his enthusiasm and big handlebar mustache.

Ladder Company 12 was a good spot for a young guy. You get all the experience you need, especially in fighting fires in high-rise buildings. He knows that getting to people trapped above a fire was an absolute bitch, but a great challenge, too. There is nothing like the rush of going to a fire in a high rise. Scary as shit, sure, but getting up there, going on the roof—maybe saving people—you can't beat that.

They're standing outside the house watch, both flicking their cigarettes to the gutter, when someone says, "Check this out. Better get ready."

■ Flip Mullen is at home, the TV on in the background. He was one of the guys who ran out of Droesch's Bar to save people when the house next door burst into flames that Christmas morning in 1966. He wouldn't become an actual firefighter for another four years. Then he'd spend 16 years with the FDNY until he was forced to retire with a back injury.

He'd been a New York City police officer. He helped keep the crowd back the day the big fire took out Curley's Hotel in Rockaway in 1968, but left to join the fire department in 1970. He joined the FDNY just a couple years after his friend, Pete Hayden. Flip went to Ladder 120 in Brownsville, Brooklyn and later to Rescue 1 in the city. Flip's assignment to 120 meant joining one of the busiest firehouses in the country. They'd get 30 or 40 calls in a single night.

Flip's family was growing. He and his wife, Rita, had seven kids. They thought it might be time to slow down a bit, take a little less risk in the day-to-day job, and transfer to the relatively quiet firehouse on Beach 116th Street in Rockaway. There'd be fires and some pretty good jobs, but it'd be nothing like Brownsville.

He was settling into the quieter life, running an ice cream route on the side, the night they answered a call on Beach 131st Street. With the fire still going, he went inside on his hands and knees to do a primary search. Crawling through the kitchen, he felt something mushy, then realized it was a dead dog. He wanted to get the dog out of the way in case they had to head back this way in a hurry. He stood and lifted 80 pounds of German shepherd. Too heavy to carry very far, Flip tossed the dog through the back window and it landed with a thud in the backyard. Alas, the German shepherd was not dead. *The Wave* and the dog's owners gave Flip credit for fighting the fire and saving the dog named Whiskey. The guys in the firehouse had some fun with the headlines, saying they weren't a bit surprised that Flip saved Whiskey. He would've saved brandy and scotch, too.

He'd make the newspaper again after trying to knock down a door to rescue someone caught in an apartment fire above a store. It looked like a fairly flimsy door, ready to go with a good shoulder. Flip, a solid guy, had the shoulders to do most doors. He got a head of steam and speared the door. He fell to the ground, thinking he had broken his back. He had actually splintered the door, but it had been fortified by two-by-fours. He got to his feet, grabbed the trapped woman, and they both rolled down the stairs to escape the flames. The woman was fine; Flip's back wasn't.

On TV, he sees the north tower of the Trade Center on fire. He starts thinking about his old canvas turnout coat, helmet, and claw tool in the basement. He might need that stuff.

■ Deputy Chief Pete Hayden has lived in Rockaway for more than 40 years. Nothing unusual about that, yet the way in which other firefighters speak his name is extraordinary. Firefighters are known to dabble in irreverence and ball-breaking. Actually, many are more than dabblers—they are absolute masters.

Sensitive about that bald spot? They'll remind you that it's there and it's getting bigger. They'll question your taste in music, women, cars, sports—you name it. You'd best develop a thick skin because they'll zero in on something. Maybe it'll be the time you drop a tool or you trip—you may be forever known as a klutz. Somehow, some way, you'll be tested. Although the banter can be harsh—especially stuff directed at Probies—many firefighters say it's just a way of saying to each other, Nobody here, nobody on this job, is better than anyone else. Everybody's got weaknesses, so we had better stick together, and don't you forget it!

Firefighters, in general, are not quick to give or take credit. After a rescue or extinguishing a roaring blaze, what does a firefighter say? He was "just doing his job." When a firefighter hears of another firefighter doing something heroic or brave, what does he say? "That guy was just doing his job, too."

It's different with Chief Hayden. When they talk about Chief Hayden, or merely mention his name, there's an unmistakable tone of respect, admiration—and sometimes awe—in their voices. It can't be the rank, although deputy chief and commander of Division 1 in Manhattan are pretty lofty titles in the FDNY. He got there after stints in Brooklyn at Engine 207, Ladder 110, and Rescue 2. He became captain at Ladder 147 in Brooklyn and then a chief in Manhattan.

If anything, a high rank can inspire resentment and suspicion among regular firefighters. Bosses are easily viewed as bureaucrats or bookworms—guys who can test well. Firefighters might look at a boss and wonder if he ever ate smoke or if he's forgotten what it's like on the front lines. One firefighter, looking at a chief at a house fire in Brooklyn, said, "That chief don't go in the fire, but he's good at checking your regulation socks and T-shirts."

No such cracks are heard about Pete Hayden. He's stayed true. Soft spoken, with an easy laugh, he's still a regular guy, though if anybody's got a right to brag, he'd be the guy.

He gained his experience when New York City seemed to be burning itself into oblivion. Today, they'd be called "urban riots." In the late 1960s and through the 1970s, there were no such descriptions. When blocks in Bushwick and Brownsville and the South Bronx went up in flames, no one called it rioting—they just called it another Friday or Saturday night for fire companies. Hayden worked in a time when he'd say "See you tomorrow!" to some friend on the job, and then never see the guy again.

Too often, there were 30 or 40 runs a night. Guys would get killed, severely burned, lose an eye, or shatter bones. Hayden had a number of close calls himself, including one at Macy's at Herald Square, when fire flashed its way through the first floor of the department store, trapping Hayden and others. They lost their way in the dark and the heat started to swallow them. Suddenly, a door opened, someone pulled him through, and he was saved but hospitalized with burns on his ears and hands. It was just one of several times he had last thoughts. Usually it was, "How's Rita gonna manage with the five kids?" He'd been a firefighter's fighter; yet, as he became part of the brass, guys would say, he still looked out for the rank and file.

This morning, Chief Hayden is in his office at division head-quarters in lower Manhattan. With all the ambient sounds in the city, and because of established flight patterns, you can't hear noise from airplanes overhead.

What is that? He goes to his office window and can't see the plane because the buildings block his view, but he knows it's a jet—probably a commercial jet. He immediately thinks that it's going to crash, and it does. He can hear the impact from his office window and knows the plane has struck one of the Twin Towers.

He says, "Let's go!" to his driver and they head to the car. The alarm comes in that a plane has hit the Trade Center. It's a clear day. It's got to be a terrorist. Any other pilot would have taken the plane into the water.

■ In Rockaway, Joe Esposito, just retired from the fire department, stands on the sidewalk of Beach Channel Drive looking across Jamaica Bay to the Manhattan skyline in the distance. He nods at someone passing on a bicycle. "Hey, look! One of the Twin Towers is on fire!"

The guy on the bike stops, squints a bit and says, "That looks like a hole in the building."

At the Harbor Health and Fitness Club, people are on stationary bikes or treadmills. Some machines face a television set with the morning news; some face out to the bay and the Manhattan skyline, allowing exercisers to see the black smoke billowing upward. Someone jokes that the tower looks like a big piece of dynamite in a cartoon. No one laughs.

The newspeople on TV have little information. In the exercise club, people are interested but continue their workouts. There is speculation that it's a commuter plane that has crashed into the tower. Someone mentions John F. Kennedy, Jr., implying the pilot was probably inexperienced or had some kind of blackout. How could you not see the Twin Towers?

The news anchor on Channel 7 theorizes that there has likely been a computer glitch of some kind at air traffic control at one of the three major airports.

In the gym, there's concerned talk: some people are obviously dead, some are going to be trapped, but there's no alarm, no dread at this point. With little new information coming from the newscasters, there's small talk about the things that have occurred at the Twin Towers since the ribbon-cutting ceremony in 1973. It started with the French guy, Phillipe Petit, who walked the tightrope between the buildings. Then there was George Willig, the guy who climbed one of the towers and had to pay a fine of $1.10—a penny for every floor. Somebody else parachuted off the roof, and someone mentions the remake of *King Kong*.

Conversation stops when someone says, "Don't forget the terrorists who tried to blow the place up in 1993."

▪ Bernie Heeran picks up the phone after a few rings, but he has to talk over the answering machine that already clicked on and is now taping the conversation. It's Charlie.

Turn on the TV, he's saying. He's trapped with scores of others on the 104th floor of the North Tower. What should we do? The smoke is really bad, he says, but there's a steady calm in his voice.

Bernie asks him about the elevators, the stairwells. You've checked them all? He's got the phone to his ear, his eyes on the television.

Charlie says he's checked everything and there seems to be no way out. Bernie tells him to go to the roof. The helicopters will come and snatch you off the roof.

Bernie hangs up, knowing he can't just sit around the house waiting.

▪ Chief Hayden had seen the hole in the ground. He would never forget the massive, football field-sized crater blown into the basement and foundation of the Trade Center in 1993 by a terrorist's bomb. He'd been a battalion chief at the time and, since peering into the deep hole, he had an acute appreciation of how the Trade Center had a perverse appeal to crazies and terrorists. A jet plane crashing? There was no way this was an accident.

As he arrives at the north tower, he sees six or eight badly burned people right outside the building. He wonders how they got down to the lobby so quickly. He thinks that maybe they were in an elevator and the jet fuel poured down the elevator shafts. He goes to the lobby command post and learns that virtually all the building services are out—no phones, no elevators. The elevators give him pause. What if they come crashing down from a hundred floors up? They'd blow into the lobby and who knows what that would do—especially if there were jet fuel in the elevator shafts.

There's a lot to consider for Hayden, including the terrorism aspect of the situation. It makes him think that there could be a secondary device—a bomb that'll go off just as emergency responders arrive to help. He also thinks collapse is a possibility, and then there's the matter of trying to evacuate 25,000 people. He's grateful that, at least in the lobby, things are calm and under control, but upstairs—that's another matter. The fire suppression system is knocked out. The primary goal won't be putting out the fire—it'll be search and evacuate.

■ On the street, and in the air just above it, there is so much paper that it is oddly reminiscent of a ticker-tape parade. Reams of paper from the upper floors where windows have been shattered fly into the air and descend blithely to the ground.

■ Billy Heeran, Charlie's twin, works in Battery Park, just a few blocks from the Trade Center. He can't reach Charlie by phone, so he rushes to the tower on foot. He wants to run inside, but hundreds of people are running out—maybe Charlie's one of them—and he had better stay back because there's a lot of stuff falling and crashing. All these people had better watch out. A lot of shit's falling. Billy drifts back himself and winds up standing in front of the firehouse known as 10-10, looking up. He knows so many people on the 104th floor. Charlie will know what to do.

■ Palmer Doyle was supposed to be pulling the lever for himself today. Since he'd been going broke doing all this volunteer stuff for Rockaway, he figured he might as well do right by his family and get paid for some of the headaches. The city council job was there for the taking. He'd win the election, take a leave of absence from the fire department, and then make a decision down the road about returning to the fire department or sticking with politics. It didn't work out. With a zero budget and a seat-of-the-pants campaign, he never got enough signatures to get on the ballot. Still, he wants to keep his hand in things, so he volunteers to work the polls this morning for one of the candidates.

He's on his way to Breezy Point, which is 4 miles from his Rockaway Park home, when he sees the smoke pouring from the north tower. It is enough to make him say, "*Holy shit!*" and make a U-turn.

■ Even though Matt Tansey and everyone else is busy scrambling for gear, it's impossible to avoid seeing the TVs throughout the firehouse with their images of the black smoke pouring from the north tower of the World Trade Center. *Shit*. This isn't your everyday high-rise building. Although they call dispatch to get a green light to respond, the company is told to wait. Now, the firefighters stand, ready and eager, in a cluster, watching the TV screen in house watch. Then they see the shadow of the second plane.

▪ Besides running the Graybeards basketball league, Steve Stathis is a neighbor and friend of Pete Hayden and Flip Mullen. He's not a firefighter, but he is a trained emergency responder with Con Edison, the utility company. It's a serious job. Every third week, he's on 24-hour call for any environmental catastrophe, explosion, or serious accident or incident that might occur. If there is a power outage, or a transformer is hit by lightning, Steve will be there.

Another part of his job, prior to 8:48 AM on September 11, seems part science fiction and a little melodramatic. He is a member of the Con Edison Biological Chemical Weapons Response Team, a group ready to respond in emergency situations—including terrorist acts—in which chemical or germ warfare is used. To outsiders, it seems like training for a Hollywood movie, a disaster flick that will never happen in real life. Thanks to weekly updates about terrorist activities around the world, and an expert named Dick Morgan, Steve and his team find it easy to take the training seriously.

His workday starts early, around 7 AM. By 9 AM on September 11, he's already finished a meeting at the Con Ed "Learning Center" in Long Island City, just across the East River from Manhattan. As he leaves the building to drive back to his Coney Island office, he sees a group of co-workers pointing and looking in the distance at one of the Twin Towers on fire.

He knows that first responders are already there with more on the way. Dick Morgan, the terrorist expert, will be there. He might be responding himself right now if the poor vision in his left eye hadn't kept him off the fire department almost 30 years ago. His younger brother, Whipper, is on the job, and so is his son, Christian, but they'll both probably miss this one. Whipper's got the day off and he's probably surfing; Christian is at home, not scheduled to work until tomorrow. He'd just gotten clearance to return to work after getting some metal debris in his eye on a job the previous week.

He sees the second plane. It starts to circle.

What the hell is that guy doing?

■ Billy Heeran, Charlie's twin, standing in the shadows of the towers, sees the large plane coming. He and others think the plane is here to dump water on the fire. Maybe the sprinkler system is out and that's the only way they'll be able to fight the fire.

■ The guys in 12 Truck are standing around the TV, waiting. They all instinctively lean forward when the shadow of a plane crosses the screen. Then there's an explosion. The dispatcher barks, "12 Truck respond now." Like that, they're off.

Matt Tansey sits across from Mike Mullan as the truck shoots west on 19th Street for four blocks to the West Side Highway, then turns south towards lower Manhattan. Matt knows this is different. Most times, when they hurried towards a fire, they'd get shouts of encouragement and go-get-'em waves from people on sidewalks. Not today. Crowds of people stand transfixed, lining the West Side Highway, watching the two giant towers burn.

"Yo, man. Look at their faces," Tansey says to Mullan, sitting in the jump seat. On the way, at different spots, a couple of people look away from the towers for an instant at the guys on the truck.

Matt knows what they're thinking. They're thinking, you poor bastards. You've got to go into those buildings.

■ Bernie Heeran can't wait any longer for another call from Charlie. He hurries to his car, then speeds into Brooklyn to his old firehouse, Engine 281 on Cortelyou Road. He figures nobody'll be allowed into Manhattan unless they're on a rig or in some emergency vehicle.

■ Tommy Carroll gets on the rig at Engine 210, but not as a chauffeur. Turns out, they already had a chauffeur, so he's put on the line instead. When scheduling was done, there was the possibility that another apparatus—a maxi water, which is a descendant of the super pumper—would arrive and then they'd need a second chauffeur. Now, there's no waiting around for another engine. They're already heading into the city.

Just a few minutes earlier, Tommy and the other firefighters were watching the smoke pour from the north tower on a television set at the firehouse after a 1060—a major emergency—came in over the department radio. From the rig sailing along a service road adjacent to the Brooklyn–Queens Expressway (BQE), they can see the burning tower and the rest of lower Manhattan across the East River. From this angle, at this moment, it doesn't look that bad. Tommy turns to another firefighter to say there's plenty of smoke but . . .

"Holy shit!"

Tommy spins in his seat at the cry. A young guy, maybe three or four years on the job, eyes popping out of his head, is pointing his finger towards Manhattan. Balls of fire in quick succession explode out of the south tower.

The sons of bitches have timers. They're setting off bombs. Tommy knows it's terrorists, but he and the others don't know yet that a second plane has just ripped through the other tower. They don't know the facts; they just know it's bad. Tommy can see a gaping hole in the building and can make out individual floors behind a curtain of flames. This is different. Basement jobs, building collapses, some real roaring fires—he'd seen plenty in 17 years, but this . . . this was going to be a long day, or the last day.

The rig jounces towards the Battery Tunnel, but the driver misses the turn and has to swing around the toll plaza to find an entry lane. The minute delay allows Tommy's regular ladder company, 105, to enter the tunnel just ahead of 210.

So many emergency vehicles are trying to get into Manhattan that there's a clog in the tunnel. Hot, heavy air makes the tunnel feel like a sauna, though this one offers no healthful benefits. This sauna is full of car and truck fumes. It's oppressive and claustrophobic enough that firefighters want to abandon their rigs and run towards the opening on the Manhattan side. Officers tell them to stay put.

■ It's about 9 AM and George Johnson is scratching sleep out of his eyes. He's usually up by now, but the Giants' game had ended late, and he was still wiped out from the rugby match against the Jersey team when he had to play winger in the first half and hooker in the second. Hard enough that he had to play two very different positions, and harder that they had gotten spanked. Not a good way to start the fall season.

From his apartment window in Rockaway Beach, he can see the Atlantic Ocean. The waves are huge and clean. The surf he and a half dozen other Rockaway guys found in Indonesia and Nicaragua on a surfing odyssey they'd gone on a few months back had spoiled him, but today, the Rockaway surf looked world class. It's going to be great. He'd skip the morning shower and get wet in the ocean.

On his way to the kitchen for a drink of water, he absent-mindedly turned on the TV. One of the Twin Towers had charcoal smoke pouring from its side near the top of the building. "What a job that's going to be," he thought. The news anchor had little information.

In the kitchen, a bit of sleep still in his eyes, he's not sure but he thinks he's just heard the guy on television say, "I know we've been told that this crash is contained to Tower One, but I just saw a giant fireball come out of Tower Two."

"What?"

The guy on TV asks a colleague, "Is there something wrong with the navigational instruments at the airports?"

George shouts at the television, "You stupid fuck! It's *terrorism!*"

He calls his brother, Mike, and tells him they've got to get to work. His brother Bob calls and says the same thing.

As he starts to run out the door, the phone rings again. Somebody from the firehouse yells for him to "Pick up Fish! Pick up Fish!" George knows that means Mike King, another firefighter, who everybody calls "Fish." Fish doesn't have a car and will need a ride.

George jumps in his car and the gas needle is on empty. He lets out a frustrated scream and then heads to the gas station for five bucks of gas.

■ Flip Mullen throws on his turnout coat, grabs his old and dented helmet, and his claw tool. He hopes they haven't closed the bridges out of Rockaway yet. Three blocks from his house, he sees a police patrol car parked at the bay wall and two cops watching the burning towers. Flip hops out of his car and asks the cops for a ride. Seconds later, he's in a police car with a sergeant doing 90 MPH over the bridge into Brooklyn.

The sergeant has to get back to Rockaway, so he drops Flip at the entrance to the Belt Parkway. It's good enough for Flip; he knows he'll be able to hitch a ride with somebody. Sure enough, two cops in a Chevy Tahoe see him in his antique gear. They pull over and tell him to jump in.

■ Chief Hayden and other top brass are giving instructions to arriving firefighter companies, though there's suddenly more confusion because some are coming from a staging area outside while others are off-duty freelancers rushing in. There's even confusion about which tower is which: "Tower One is the north tower—does everyone know that? Post a sign."

Debris is falling from the towers and making terrifying sounds, like bombs. Everyone is flinching. They soon realize that human beings are among the falling debris. Hayden has to stay focused.

"We've got a report of people trapped on 71," he tells an officer. "Bodies are falling. We've got to get these people out. You gotta go get 'em."

In some of the men's eyes, he can read something he doesn't want to read. They don't say anything, but their eyes say they know this might be it . . . they might not come back. Hayden's got to swallow, stay focused. These guys, his guys, are something. You want to talk about brave? Guys with courage? Look no further.

Here are plenty with raw, extreme concern and fear, yet they don't hesitate. They nod at the orders and head upstairs.

Some of the fire department commissioners and chiefs leave to assess matters from a different perspective and to establish an outside command post. Hayden stays at what is now an operations post. People are steadily moving out of the building. Even below the point of impact and where the fire is roaring, it's a long way down to the lobby. They've got to move faster.

■ Monsignor Martin Geraghty is in a dentist's chair in Five Towns, just steps into Nassau County over the Rockaway border, having two teeth extracted. Although the first plane has hit the north tower, there's no point in stopping the dental work. He and the dentist agree that it's probably some daredevil who tried something stupid with a small jet.

His mouth is numb and full of blood when the second plane crashes. The dentist hurries to finish. Geraghty has never had teeth pulled before. He had taken the advice of others: plan an easy day and cancel appointments because there's going to be discomfort. He gets out of the chair and heads back to St. Francis in Belle Harbor. This day was supposed to be about teeth. He tosses the gauze from his mouth. It's not going to be about teeth.

■ Bernie Heeran, retired firefighter and father of Charlie, arrives at the firehouse in Brooklyn too late—the engine has already been called to lower Manhattan. Figuring there's little to do here, he heads back to Rockaway. He'll go to St. Francis de Sales Church and plead.

■ Trucks from other companies are blocking the streets, so the rig pulls to a stop just south of Stuyvesant High School, a couple of blocks north of the towers. Matt Tansey is not scared. The adrenaline makes his legs feel ready and strong. He knows he'll be going in and maybe have to climb the stairs all the way up. Gotta stay focused.

Matt and his company hurry to an operations post. Suddenly, it's easy to lose focus. All sorts of shit is coming down: part of a beam and what looks like some of the exterior wall of the building lay in the street. Office equipment falls from the sky, some of it coming down as balls of fire. Then bodies: human beings falling from 1,000 feet, some of them on fire. He doesn't want to look. Matt, absolutely terrified—never close to being this scared in his life—tries to maneuver past the debris and death before him. A chunk of the building the size of a piano slams to the ground just 10 feet from him.

He has no choice but to look up. He's supposed to go to the lobby of the Marriott Hotel at the base of the south tower, maybe just a few hundred yards away, but it feels like he's traveling in slow motion. He doesn't care that the building is on fire; he wants shelter from these men in their business suits coming right at him. Something about them in their suits makes it even more sickening.

They start down, not so fast at first. He has to track them so he doesn't get hit. They seem to be floating. Then, just like that, they're coming fast, and he can hear them coming. It's a low scream at first, and it builds and builds. For a split second, he can make out the features on their faces. The scream is piercing now and then they hit. Jesus, it's actually the people screaming, all the way until they hit. Until they explode.

Christ, he has friends up there.

■ In Rockaway, Palmer Doyle gets ready to drive to his firehouse—Engine 254 in Brooklyn—but first stops at St. Francis de Sales School and tells the principal he wants to see his kids. She tells him that she thinks it's best if the kids stay in their classes until more is known about what's going on.

"Sister, I might not see my kids again. I want to give them a hug and a kiss *right now.*"

■ Some parents are at home or work close by, so they start pulling their kids out of school. They don't know what's happening; all

they know is that they want their kids—*now*—but that only makes
other kids who remain in school scared and unsettled.

Why aren't my parents coming for me?

■ A man sprints through the sand, then into the ocean up to his
knees, waving frantically at three or four surfers. He gets their
attention and starts pointing behind himself in the direction of the
city. Waving both hands over his head, he urges them in. They are
firefighters and they're needed.

■ George Johnson spots Mike King on the side of the road in
Breezy Point, waiting for the ride. They shoot across the Marine
Park Bridge into Brooklyn, then run every red light on Flatbush
Avenue until they get to Engine 255, Ladder 157—their firehouse
on Rogers Avenue. Nearly three dozen off-duty firefighters are
assembled, and they pile into an assortment of pick-up trucks,
vans, and a Suburban.

■ Tommy Carroll, with Engine 210, finally makes its way out of
the tunnel. After a couple of minutes, 210 is waved to a staging
area on West Street, just across from the burning towers. Tommy
steps out of the rig and nearly on top of a torso. He wonders if it
came from the plane. Things are definitely bad if no one has
stopped to remove a body. He takes another look, still trying to
compute what he sees: no arms, no legs, torn as if a wildcat got to
it, but definitely a human torso.

Fire companies and apparatus from all over the city are arriving. West Street is swarming with uniformed responders. As they
check in at the command post in front of the American Express
building, Tommy and the others from 210 learn it was a second
plane that hit the south tower. It is here that Chief of Department
Pete Ganci, Deputy Commissioner Bill Feehan, and other chiefs
are organizing the dozens of firefighters on hand, and designing a
strategy for rescue and fire control.

Tommy knows Feehan from Rockaway and Breezy Point. Feehan used to rent a bungalow in Rockaway Beach and now owns a

summer home in Breezy. The guy's a pro. He's held every rank in the fire department.

Tommy feels better knowing Ganci's here, too. He's the highest ranking uniformed officer in the FDNY. No ivory tower about this guy. He's an expert on all things job-related, and he likes nothing more than to be shoulder to shoulder with his troops. Hands-on guy, all the way. Tommy has known him since he was the chief of Battalion 57.

At the same time, Tommy realizes he doesn't really know any of the other guys he's working with today. When you get detailed, it's a luck of the draw who you might share a shift with—sometimes you'll work with a bunch of guys you've known for years; sometimes the group is full of strangers that perhaps you'll know better by the end of the shift or perhaps not. Tommy had shown up at 210 and was immediately on the rig heading into the city. A couple of the guys looked familiar, but he couldn't say for sure. He'd been detailed to 210 before, but it had been at least a year. Now, this wasn't the time or place for break-the-ice conversation.

As it happens, he finds himself standing with the guys from his regular house—219 and 105—at the staging area near a traffic island on West Street. Frankie Palumbo, Dennis O'Berg, and Henry Miller look ready. He glances around to get his bearings. The towers are before him; to his back is the open mouth of a garage under the American Express building.

Tommy is carrying oxygen bottles, roll-up hoses, and fittings to connect the hoses to standpipes, expecting at any second to get the go-ahead to hit the stairs. He and Tommy Kelly, one of his regular guys with 105, exchange looks. This is fucked up.

Kelly looks up at the tower, then down to the street and back at Tommy. "What are we supposed to put on this?" The implication is clear: they're going to need something more than water to put this fire out.

Then it starts raining people. Eighty to a hundred firefighters on West Street are stunned. One after another, bodies are falling . . . from each tower. Some look like they're coming down in slow motion. Tommy can see their faces and then he hears the sounds.

One sounds like a shotgun blast; another like an oversized water balloon; another like an air gun; another like a car crash. A single, ugly noise, then a jarring staccato and *rat-tat-tat-tat*.

Tommy grabs hold of a young firefighter's shoulder and turns him. "You don't need to see this." He raises his voice to other guys who suddenly seem a lot younger than he remembers them. "Guys, why don't you look towards the river 'til we get our orders. Look away. You'll hear them anyway." Some of the men seem grateful for the suggestion and turn. Even for those who don't—or can't—pull their eyes away, duty soon calls.

Dennis Cross, the battalion chief in the 57 in Brooklyn who is now acting as deputy chief on the scene, shouts out the initial assignments. "Okay. 105 and 132, let's go!" He shouts the numbers of several other companies, causing men to cluster for a moment, then head towards the tower.

Everyone here knows that firefighting is about teamwork. Sure, some guys like to be the first ones in, but they do so knowing they have a network of support—men and women making sure their hoses are supplied with water, ready to bail them out if they find trouble. Engine and truck companies have a natural rivalry: engine companies joke that, while truck guys go to medal ceremonies, engine guys go for skin grafts. In the big picture, though, they know it's about teamwork. Heroic rescues and successful rescue attempts stem from everyone pitching in.

It's likely Cross picked 105 and 132 because those companies are in his battalion. He's simply familiar with the companies and their officers. He knows most firefighters want to work, not stand around, and not be relief. He's not necessarily doing them a favor, handing them a bone; he happens to know the captains, Vinny Brunton and Tommy Haskell. They're good and so are their guys. They get the call.

■ There's no way down. Charlie Heeran is certain of that. He tells a group of colleagues that his father's a firefighter and that they'll send helicopters to make rescues from the roof. On the north side of the building, New York Police Department (NYPD) helicopters hover, trying to get closer.

▪ Billy Heeran runs towards 125 Broad Street, where his brother, Sean, works. As soon as he enters the lobby, he sees Sean. They blurt out at each other, asking about Charlie. Neither has been able to reach him.

▪ Flip Mullen and the two cops enter the Battery Tunnel tube, which is normally reserved for outgoing traffic. The right-hand lane is cleared so emergency responders can get through, but it's slow going because so many are trying to get to the scene. There's a trickle of traffic still leaving, although the tunnel has been officially closed to regular traffic. Some impatient drivers swing into the lane to get past the snarl, but then must swerve back to avoid the vehicles still trying to get out of Manhattan. On the elevated walkway that hugs the wall—usually used by maintenance workers and police—there's a crush of civilians trying to escape.

▪ Matt Tansey, looking up and down, up and down, keeps running. The lobby's just ahead. Damn, he wants to get into that burning tower in the worst way. Suddenly, he stumbles, then slips and falls. He's hands first on the ground, in the watery remains of a jumper. He glances about, surrounded by office materials and splattered humans. *Fuck.* He's got to get up and get the hell out of here. It looks like these people went through a wood chipper.

Steps from the lobby, Matt sees another man in a suit hurtling towards the street. There's a Lincoln Town Car parked at the curb. Matt flinches as the man slams directly in the middle of the roof of the car. The glass explodes; the front and back of the big sedan fold upward and together like a suitcase. When he finally gets inside, there's a brief moment of relief. Some guys ask, Did you see this? Did you see that? Others are too shaken to speak at all.

He had survived the run to the lobby just to be told it was time to get to work. Ladder companies are lined up on one side and engine companies are on the other. Matt and his company are instructed to start on the 15th floor and do a sweep of the top floors of the Marriott for any civilians that might still be inside. The Marriott, a 22-story building on the west side of Two World Trade Center, is essentially part of the tower's base. Through the Marriott, you can use walkways and bridges to get to other parts of the World Trade Center—a complex of seven buildings including the Twin Towers.

Matt and the others climb the 15 floors, carrying anywhere from 60 to 100 pounds of equipment, and begin banging on doors and listening for sounds of life. There's at least a small touch of familiarity creeping back in his mind. This is something firefighters do: they make searches and rescues. They try every room on the 15th, then hit the stairs again and start on 16. Matt is not surprised to find the place empty. This hotel would probably accommodate adults—businesspeople who would have the sense to get out. Kids are the ones who hide from fires. You never know, though, so you keep checking.

They check every floor, all the way to the 18th. They've seen no one. Four more floors to go. They climb the stairs to the 19th and, just as they swing open the door, the south tower collapses. A black, roaring, hurricane-force wind slams Matt and the others back, heaving them against the walls and down the flight of stairs. They're like loose jellybeans in a jar, bouncing down the concrete stairs.

■ Kelly nods at Tommy, then grabs a spare oxygen bottle and joins Brunton, Chipura, Miller, and the others from 105 and 132 as they head towards the south tower—the whole time looking skyward and preparing to dodge falling debris or plunging humans.

If Tommy had taken the detail across the floor instead of accepting the assignment to 226 and then to 210, he'd be going to work. Instead, Tommy wonders if it's time to relax, that there won't be much to do until he's called to relieve the companies that have just gone in. Sixty or 70 other firefighters still standing there probably have the same thought.

It's a thought that doesn't last long. Another chief shouts that there is a report of another plane. Somebody says they hit the Pentagon and another plane crashed in Pennsylvania. *Huh?* What the fuck's in Pennsylvania? Is that what the chief is saying? There was another plane, or is it two? Is there another plane coming this way?

"Here it comes!"

Deafening thunder rolls through the streets. He can't see it, but with the noise, Tommy thinks a jet is about to crash and explode on top of him. Other firefighters break for the underground garage and Tommy pushes a stunned rookie in the same direction.

Although Tommy thinks it's a plane, it's actually the south tower coming down—and fast. The top of the building (1,368 feet above where he's standing) will slam into the ground in less than nine seconds. It will take a couple more seconds for the debris to spread. He's got to run for his life and he's got about 12 seconds. Rushing down the garage ramp with the crowd, Tommy is about 25 yards inside when he opts to take cover behind a cement column.

■ Chief Hayden hears a growing roar, like a jet plane, maybe a fleet of jets. Anything you can compare it to, this is worse. He glances towards a window and sees a black wave of cloud and heat charging towards him. This is it. Oh boy, Rita and the five kids.

He runs towards the underside of the escalators. The gust of dust and debris envelops, grabs, and lifts Hayden off the floor.

■ The Battery Tunnel darkens with dust and debris. Civilians covered in dust—some with blood running down their faces—run on the road and the elevated walkway. Traffic is at a standstill. For now, no vehicles are being allowed into Manhattan.

Flip Mullen is out of the Chevy Tahoe, helping some people get into ambulances. An off-duty firefighter on a motorcycle weaves his way through the tunnel, but Flip stops him to say that he won't be able to go much farther—they're letting nobody through. He knows a shortcut to the Brooklyn Bridge.

Flip, 57 years old—holding his claw tool and wearing a T-shirt, dungarees, and his fire helmet—hops onto the back of the motorcycle. As they fly along the BQE, Flip shakes his head. Shit, he left his old turnout coat in the Tahoe.

They join emergency responders of all kinds in a race over the Brooklyn Bridge into Manhattan. Thousands of scared people are leaving the city on foot; some look like they're covered in flour.

■ Billy and Sean Heeran, still inside the lobby at 125 Broad Street, don't know what the hell to do. Charlie's in the north tower; he's got to get out. *Now.*

■ Steve Stathis is trying to get back to the Coney Island office of Con Edison, but is stuck in the traffic on the BQE across from lower Manhattan. Traffic can be heavy on this road at any hour, but now it's truly horrendous as it fills with trucks and cars that have fled Manhattan or were turned away before heading in. Of course, there's considerable rubbernecking as drivers are mesmerized by the fire and smoke flowing from the towers.

Steve squints a bit. Something has drawn his eyes to the south tower. He can't believe it, but it seems to be quivering near the top. Then it implodes.

How many people—how many friends—just got killed? Ashen, in shock, his eyes shift wearily to the other tower.

CHAPTER 3

Ground Zero

June 1922

Just days after the devastation, New York's mayor came to Rockaway for the first time. The mayor, local politicians, police, and merchants championed a "return to normalcy" campaign, hoping residents could somehow move past the horror. The year was 1922.

Arverne—a flourishing section of Rockaway, with showy residences, bungalows, first-rate hotels, and boardinghouses—was still hurrying to accommodate the summer crowds that had started to arrive on Memorial Day, two weeks earlier. Businessmen erected new signs and stocked shelves in anticipation of another boom year. Painters and carpenters were still sprucing up boardinghouses and hotels as early vacationers headed for the new boardwalk and beach.

Rockaway as a whole was thriving. Boardinghouses and hotels, depending on their accommodations, were filled with the wealthy or the working class. Truly inexpensive vacationing was available at a number of "tent cities." Scores of tents, each one nearly the size of a bungalow, were lined in rows just off the boardwalk on various blocks.

Although Arverne had been a popular destination for more than a decade—drawing stars such as Sophie Tucker, Mae West, and Isadora Duncan to vacation or entertain—the area was also the year-round home to a thriving, growing Jewish community. Derech Emunoh, or the Road to Faith, erected in 1905, was the synagogue that hundreds attended. The synagogue became known for its architecture as well as its active congregation. Although the interior adhered to Sephardic ritual, the exterior was unusual with its large, arched windows and shingled, decidedly Georgian Revival style.

Good, quick train service brought people from Brooklyn and Pennsylvania Station in Manhattan to the hotels, beaches, restaurants, and non-gambling casinos. An 800-seat theater abutted the boardwalk, affording visitors fresh air and expansive views of the Atlantic. It was a place to be.

Like a number of hotels, the Nautilus Hotel on Beach 59th Street was getting a new coat of paint on Thursday afternoon, June 15. Painters were busy on a second-story veranda, some smoking as they worked. Apparently, a discarded cigarette or match wedged between floorboards, and went unnoticed until a man from across the street, himself painting a bungalow, shouted that the veranda was on fire.

The painters working on the Nautilus tried to check the blaze, but the dry wood-frame structure was excellent tinder. A strong wind blew in off the Atlantic, fanning the fire and sending embers to other buildings in the area. The neighborhood was a firefighter's nightmare: wood-framed buildings squeezed next to each other, all without fire walls. In no time, a four-block area—from ocean to bay—was on fire.

Residents formed bucket brigades, frantically awaiting Engine 265, which was regularly stationed just a few blocks away at Beach 64th Street. However, 265 was on a call and the fire took advantage. Engine 266, stationed at Beach 86th Street (27 blocks away), was the first to arrive. The fire was already out of control.

Over the next five hours, 68 fire companies from Queens and parts of Brooklyn, Manhattan, and Nassau County made their way to Arverne. Once there, to attack the fire, some companies weaved their way through walls of flame, as both sides of the street burned. Low water pressure supplied by a private company—just a slight improvement over the feeble sprays used on the Seaside fire of 1892—made hose work futile and the wind stayed strong. Five fireboats worked the edges of the fire from the bay.

Running through thin corridors of daylight with flames on each side, hundreds of people sought refuge on the beach, carrying or dragging what possessions they could. Soon, however, the ocean tide rolled closer and closer, threatening to wash away the belongings they had saved.

A red glare in the sky over Arverne was visible for miles. On the ground, firefighters covered in soot, smoke, water, and sweat fought flames and ran into buildings, searching for people trapped inside.

Fearing the fire would continue to spread, Deputy Chief Smokey Joe Martin called in a dynamite crew, but the explosives were not needed. The efforts of hundreds of firefighters and volunteer residents like Saul Rosenblatt and William Altholtz finally brought the fire under control.

Soldiers from the 58th Coastal Artillery were dispatched and given orders to shoot looters. Although police made a number of arrests, the soldiers didn't fire a shot. Instead, they looked at the numbed, homeless throng and were reminded of the people who lined the streets as they made their way back from the French and Belgian fronts in World War I.

Ten hours of fire wreaked unfathomable damage: 150 homes, 10 hotels, an orphanage, and the Coast Guard Station were wiped out. Engine 265 had answered its call, then raced to the big fire; it, too, caught fire and was destroyed. Three thousand people were left homeless overnight.

Neighbors in Arverne and Rockaway Beach opened their homes, cramming in hundreds of refugees who needed shelter. Hundreds more slept on the beach, with blankets supplied by a local Girl Scouts troop, the Red Cross, and other locals.

Early the next morning, stunned residents and firefighters looked out on a forest of chimneys. The brick structures survived the blaze and rose out of the blackened earth like petrified trees or lanky headstones. There would be no need for real headstones; death was somehow avoided. Sixty people, mostly firefighters, were treated at the scene for minor injuries; just a handful went to the hospital.

The Wave *newspaper reported "numberless" stories of locals who assisted in the cause. Police officer Edward Gallagher and taxicab driver Leroy Andrews pulled two women and a young girl, overcome by smoke, from a burning cottage. A 15-year-old girl, Odessa Anderson, clad in just a bathing suit, slipped past police to help refugees remove their belongings. She, too, helped a mother and baby get out of a burning building. Leon Wetzler, a bottler, brought cases of ginger ale to thirsty firefighters.*

Telephone operators—few residents had private phones—relayed messages to friends and relatives across the country. Mary McKenna and Ida

Cohen brought sandwiches to the refugees on the beach. McKenna recalled the threatening tide. "If the Lord is angry and driving us all into the water, better we go on a full stomach." Nervous, relieved laughter broke out when McKenna made her remark.

Also remarkable was the comment by a wizened firefighter, saluting Mrs. McKenna: "I remember her doing the same 30 years ago," recalling her efforts at the great Seaside fire of 1892.

Mayor George Hylan and Fire Commissioner John Drennan visited the fire-swept area and immediately called for improvements in firefighting equipment, water mains, hydrants, building codes, and public awareness of fire hazards. Editorials from The Wave, *the* Brooklyn Daily Eagle, *the* Evening Sun, *and the* Evening Telegram *called for the same.*

There would be measures taken to improve firefighting and safety, to be sure. Yet, within weeks of the fire, hammers, saws, and the general din of new construction in Arverne overwhelmed the outcry.

September 2001

On the morning of September 11, 2001, there were 496 active firefighters living in Rockaway and hundreds of retired ones. If you count those who rent houses for the summer, the active number is well over 500. Add dozens more if you count guys who spend many summers here as lifeguards. Most live on the west end of the peninsula—the suburban-like, 6-mile stretch, which includes neighborhoods called Rockaway Beach, Rockaway Park, Belle Harbor, Neponsit, Roxbury, and Breezy Point.

It's common for locals to say they're "from Rockaway," no matter where on the peninsula they live. The name "Rockaway" is of uncertain origin, though it's commonly believed to be a corruption of the word "Rechouwhacky"—a Native American word that either referred to a tribe of the Canarsie Indians or the place itself. Dutch and English settlers used variations, including "Rechquakkie" and "Rackeaway." Eventually, quirks of dialect created "Rockaway" and that proved to be easy, popular, and lasting.

Now, the entire peninsula is often referred to as "The Rock-aways," which seems appropriate and encompassing because, in addition to the mid-peninsula neighborhoods of Rockaway Beach and Rockaway Park, the eastern tip is called Far Rockaway and the western end goes by Rockaway Point. However, the plural name "The Rockaways" is really an outsider's appellation. Locals will generally say they're "from Rockaway" or, if they're sure to which neighborhood they belong—no easy task—they might say Breezy Point or Belle Harbor or Far Rockaway, but they'll never say they're from "The Rockaways." The post office and the news-casters will refer to the whole peninsula or even parts on the west end as "Far Rockaway," but that doesn't sit well with people unless they're actually from the section rightfully called Far Rockaway.

There are more than 20 named neighborhoods on the penin-sula, which can be as narrow as three blocks between ocean and bay. At its widest, just a mile separates the salt water of the Atlan-tic Ocean and Jamaica Bay. Neighborhood borderlines are gener-ally unclear, and some have been known to shift a bit because of clever real estate marketers or a school board that drew a line somewhere.

While there is no unanimous opinion about where Rockaway Beach ends and Rockaway Park begins, everyone from the locals to the Ramones—the Hall of Fame rock band—agree: Playland, with its famous roller coaster, closed for good in 1987, was in Rockaway Beach. Discord also abounds concerning the point at which Rockaway Park ends and Belle Harbor begins. If you want to start a fight, it's not all that difficult to find someone willing to bloody your nose—or at least wave a property deed in your face—about the boundary argument. Yet, most people in these neighborhoods willingly accept the generalized "Rockaway" as the place they call home.

The public beaches are another matter. Come summer, east of Beach 116th Street, lifeguards will tell you that demarcations run along tribal lines. If you see little kids in underpants, it's a Puerto Rican beach; if you see grown men in their underpants, it's a

Russian beach. One veteran of many summers on a lifeguard chair says, "The surfer's beach is easy. You got surfboards and wet suits. The Irish beach, they bring coolers. The Puerto Ricans bring hibachis. The Italians bring warm Heinekens and provolone. The Brazilians? They just bring dental floss bikinis. That ain't a bad gig to get."

Off the sand, most neighborhoods bleed into each other, although Roxbury and Breezy Point—two communities on the far west end—are separated from other Rockaway neighborhoods by Riis Park Beach and Fort Tilden, a military base turned federal park.

A few decades ago, the Rockaway peninsula was an essential part of coastal defense. Nike missiles turned on their launchers like javelins inside the fort. Now, piping plovers and common terns play on the dunes along a mile of isolated beach, as poignantly beautiful as Provincetown or Hither Hills. If Rockaway's a little known New York community, Fort Tilden is an absolute secret—a mystery even to a large number of people who live on the peninsula. Although many enjoy the athletic fields in the front area of the fort, few take time to explore the 300 acres tucked in the back, near the ocean.

Beach grasses and goldenrod stabilize the dunes at the coastline and block much of the wind, salt, and sand, allowing other plants to grow in areas behind the dunes. A surprising coastal woodland exists where army jeeps once rolled and service men toiled. Through white poplar, Japanese black pine, and holly trees, you can still spot bunkers and remnants of supply huts. Since the fort became a park in 1973, a lot of vegetation has grown on its own, but some of the trees had already taken root and were planted with a purpose: to camouflage gun positions.

Though you'll no longer find the guns, you might find raccoons, possums, jackrabbits, garter snakes, and a vast assortment of birds. You can get full appreciation of this secret refuge if you climb the Harris Battery—a man-made hill that once housed a 16-inch gun. There are wooden plank steps on the side, which allow a climb to the top. From up there, you see the infinite Atlantic, the entire sweep of the great New York harbor, the majestic Verrazano Narrows Bridge, and the Silver Gull Beach Club where Matt Dillon filmed *The Flamingo Kid*. If you turn your back on the Atlantic, you see lower Manhattan. When the Twin Towers were there and if the light was right, you'd be reminded of *The Wizard of Oz*'s Emerald City.

If you turn, facing east, you see in the distance the green of a small golf course, a horse stable for mounted federal police and Engine 329—the only buildings on the street between Fort Tilden and Riis Park. It's a pleasant spot for one of the quieter firehouses in the FDNY.

◼ The earth is rattling. Some of the firefighters continue running down the ramp to lower levels. Some bolt through a doorway that leads to a stairwell. Tommy crouches deeper behind the column, squeezing tight to two other people. The roaring noise rolls down the ramp at them followed by a black blast of hot wind. He'd left his oxygen bottles on the street and now chokes on the hot, dusty air.

The garage is in complete, utter darkness. More heat rolls in. Tommy's got time to think, Shit. We're gonna roast right here. He thinks the heat from the plane and its jet fuel are going to turn the garage into an oven. Last thoughts: It was a bad idea to duck behind this column. Jesus, I hope the baby-sitter doesn't mind staying with the kids until Eileen gets home.

The noise slowly subsides, but the blackness covers the garage like felt. A voice, stunned and bewildered, rings out from somewhere. "What the *fuck*?"

Tommy can't see a thing, but he feels in one piece. He calls out, "I'm on the wall over here."

Other voices echo through the blackness. "How do you get out of here? I can't see shit."

"Follow my voice," Tommy yells. "Find a wall." They always tell you that when you're in a fire, you want to come out the way you came in, so Tommy is going to back up the ramp. Right now, it doesn't seem like the best option. It's so dark that he figures the mouth of the garage has been sealed shut by debris.

A hand tugs at his arm. "I can't breathe. I got asthma." Tommy figures it's one of the guys he squeezed in with behind the column. He grabs hold of the man's bare elbow, tells him he'll be okay, and then urges him to follow up the ramp. "Stay to the wall."

It's one foot at a time. It's so dark, you feel—even though you're going uphill—the ramp might suddenly end and you'll fall into an abyss. Tommy keeps hold of the man who is really struggling with his breath. It suddenly occurs to Tommy that the guy's not wearing bunker gear—he's a civilian. "What were you doing here?"

"I'm with the EPA [Environmental Protection Agency]."

"Well, do something about this air, will ya?" Tommy says. The guy lets go with a cough—or a laugh—as they continue to inch along.

Pausing for a moment to look back, Tommy can't see anything except darkness lightly speckled by useless flashlights—chalk dots on a blackboard, their beams simply unable to extend.

It's quiet as they climb the ramp, except for an occasional life-affirming burst from somebody—some exultation that, holy shit, they were alive.

The wall ends and they have to stop, not sure where to go from here. Tommy reaches out with his hands like a puzzled blind man. He can't see and the footing is strange, too. It feels like soft snow.

Between coughs, the guy from the EPA says, "I think that's a leaf. I think we're outside."

Flicks of light start to pierce the blackness. The guy was right: that *was* a leaf hanging from a small tree. The black curtain starts to lift, turning the area into something a bit easier to discern. All of this shit's in his eyes, but he can now see the street, dust and debris everywhere. Is that a rig on fire?

Tommy finds some oxygen bottles under inches of dust and soot, and gives air to the EPA guy, then uses another bottle of air to blow some of the dust out of his own eyes and ears.

■ The sound ends as abruptly as it came. Lifted, then thrown to the floor, Chief Hayden is surprised to find himself alive. Near the escalators, he finds the body of Father Mychal Judge, the fire department chaplain. Hayden wants to cry—Judge was such a good man—but there's no time for mourning. He and other firefighters carry him outside to the other side of the building where other firefighters lift the lifeless body and carry it towards a nearby church.

Hayden's not sure what happened. He doesn't know if it was a bomb, a third plane, or a partial collapse. Are they still under attack? He's got to get to the outside command post.

Besides Judge and others, Dick Morgan—the man who taught so many others at Con Edison about the dangers of terrorism and had arrived in the tower this morning—is dead.

■ Matt Tansey's on his back on a stairwell landing. He doesn't know if he's fallen two or three flights. It's impossible to see, nearly impossible to breath. There's a long, silent pause, then the radios go wild with calls for help.

Matt and the other guys call out to each other, "You okay?"

Before they have any real chance to orient themselves, the thick concrete wall lining the stairwell splits like paper, sending in murky light. Here comes the wind again, like the last time. It seems the same evil wind is coming back for them. Coming through the cracks at them.

There's quick agreement among the guys. "Let's get the fuck out of here!" They bolt down the steps, grabbing the railing and swinging themselves down entire flights. They keep charging, jumping, running down flight after flight—10th floor . . . ninth floor . . . eighth . . . seventh . . . sixth. Then they stop. There are no more stairs. Beneath them is 60 feet of open space, rubble, and burning gas lines—a cliff towards death.

There's no point in standing here, so they start towards the far southwest side of the building, climbing past heaps of debris and caved-in walls. Stairwells are blocked or have collapsed on this side as well. The front of the building is essentially gone. Matt peers down on crushed Emergency Medical Service (EMS) buses, fire engines, and trucks. They're going to have to rappel down. Problem is, the rescue rope was lost when they all went tumbling. Someone says they can tie the roll-up hoses they're carrying to a beam, and get down that way. Matt knows they're too high up for that.

While still trying to figure out an escape, a Mayday comes in over the radio from a firefighter trapped on the 18th floor. "Okay, stay here," Lieutenant Petti says. He and Angel Juarbe, who this morning was searching for the house to buy with his contest winnings, say, "We'll try to reach the guy by going up the same stairwell we were thrown down, and we'll come back with the rescue rope."

■ Chief Hayden is outside now on West Street, looking for the command post he knew the other top chiefs had set up sometime earlier. He's with another chief, Sal Cassano, who had also survived the blast of heat and wind that ripped through the lobby of the north tower moments before. The command post is supposed to be on Liberty and Vesey Streets, but they see that it's actually been set up a bit south, just on the other side of the pedestrian walkway or the North Bridge, which connects the cluster of buildings known as the World Trade Center and the cluster of buildings on the other side of West Street known as the World Financial Center. They start that way, fully comprehending for the first time that the south tower has completely fallen.

■ Chief Ganci appears from who knows where, and begins instructing everyone to move one block north. Tommy doesn't even know which way is north right now. He looks to his right, but he can't figure out what he's looking at. He doesn't know the south tower has collapsed.

Tommy goes back to the ramp and calls out, "210! Anybody here from 210?"

Firefighters in small clusters continue to come out of the still-dark garage. They shake their heads no, as they move past Tommy and are steered to the left, north on West Street.

As Tommy stands at the garage entrance, he turns and sees Ganci pointing and telling firefighters to head that way, that they'll be setting up one block north. Tommy again calls out, "Anybody from 210?" He's wondering why some guys head south. Maybe they can't hear Ganci. There's a lot of confusion. Ganci takes a few steps to turn some guys around and make them go the right way.

Tommy sees Timmy Grogan, a guy from the firehouse, in street clothes. He's come over from Stuy-Town, an apartment village on the East Side. Grogan tells him there's been a total recall—all firefighters have been ordered to report to their firehouses. Thousands, like Grogan, headed straight into lower Manhattan. Grogan sees that Tommy is by himself and asks him about the guys from 105. Tommy gives him the quick news about how he was detailed to 210, but that he knows his regular company got the call to go into the tower.

"Oh, shit," Grogan says. "They must've been in there when it fell."

"Fell?" Tommy looks over his shoulder, south, realizing he'd been chased into the tunnel by a skyscraper collapse. He also realizes that a lot of friends are dead.

He and Grogan start walking north, with Chief Ganci's voice behind them urging everyone to clear out. Tommy's trying to absorb it all, trying to make sense of things, but he can't. He had thought the second plane was a bomb set off by a timer. He thought a third plane had caused the building collapse. He's shaken because he thought he was going to burn to death in that garage. Now he's thinking about his friends from 219 and 105.

▪ Matt Tansey and the others can't wait to get the hell out of here. The lieutenant and Angel are making their way up to help the firefighter trapped on the 18th floor. The front of the building is ripped open. He's staring at the destruction below; another fire-fighter next to him is craning his neck, looking up.

"Here comes the other one!"

■ Chief Hayden knows this sound. In the north lobby, he didn't know, but now he knows. No one has to tell him to run or take cover. People are scattered about. Some run; some seem frozen. Chief Cassano takes cover behind a fire rig. Hayden finds partial cover under a back step on a nearby fire truck.

■ Billy and Sean Heeran are trying to figure out what they should do—if there's anything to do—when a cop runs into the lobby. "Everybody get the fuck out! The second tower is coming down!"

Now there's nothing else to do but run. They sprint towards the open air of Battery Park.

■ Tommy glances up, forcing the reality to register. There's only one tower now. "What the—"

"Here it comes!"

It's the second time today he's heard those words and he's got to run. The top of the north tower is crumbling, its innards run-ning down the sides, like lava out of a volcano. He and Grogan are in the middle of the street. There's no place to run for cover. Can they outrun 110 stories of steel and concrete?

As they sprint north, a nighttime cloud catches them as they pass Chambers Street. To their left, they glimpse a man beckoning them from a doorway of Stuyvesant High School, which sits on the banks of the Hudson River. Just as they enter, the school build-ing is enveloped in black dust.

■ Palmer Doyle and his fellow firefighters from Engine 254 are at the command post when a rumbling, thunderous sound shakes the world. The noise, almost like a physical being, surrounds them. From where? It's loud, terrifying, completely disorienting. Everyone scatters, letting instinct take them wherever. A slate cloud packed with debris rolls down the street at them like a tidal wave.

■ Matt is thinking that this must be what an avalanche is like. The sound growing faster, louder. Deafening. The sound itself might crush him. He and others run towards a cement stairwell a few yards behind them and dive underneath, Matt and another guy clutching each other. Other guys, just behind them, are gone. The building is coming down around him.

He knows he's dead. He's not praying to survive; he's hoping it doesn't hurt too much. He wants it over with. He doesn't want to know he's being crushed to death. Again, he thinks of an avalanche, only this isn't snow. He's lifted and slammed, twisted and turned, in a whirlwind of concrete and steel. His eyes are squeezed shut; he waits for the crushing pressure. Then it stops.

Silence. Implausible silence. A blackness so thick, so deep, it could only mean he's dead. Then, there's a cough from the guy he'd been clutching.

"You all right?" Matt asked between his own coughs—not sure where the guy was, but he knew he was close.

"Yeah, I think so."

Matt's got to fight his own panic. He knows the towers have fallen on him. Is he buried in 5 feet of rubble or 500? He'd been thrown about so much, he doesn't know which way is up. An avalanche. What are you supposed to do? He'd seen on some cable show that spitting could save your life. Dribble or spit, and feel the saliva run down your chin or up your nose. Gravity pulls the spit. If you're right-side up, the spit will roll down your chin; upside down, you'll feel it in your nose.

He spits out a mouthful of gook and feels it on his chin. He's prone, but twisted, his body covered with debris, the dust piled to his face. He's not sure if there's a way out. He's still blind, the darkness holding. He tries his radio, but no one answers his call.

■ The cyclone of dust and rubble settles and with it comes an unnatural silence. No street traffic, no voices—the dust soundproofs the area. Many people are hunched over, clenched, waiting for a blow that, for them, didn't come.

■ The Battery Tunnel is closed. Nobody's getting through. George Johnson and his crew of guys from Ladder 157 weave their way through a clog of traffic, then speed towards the Brooklyn Bridge. On their way across the bridge, there's not much to see—most of lower Manhattan is obscured by smoke and dust. They exit the bridge and park the truck on the sidewalk near City Hall. George looks out on a surreal world . . . like a nuclear winter, snowing dust.

■ *Shit.* Matt can't reach anyone on the radio and he knows he's got to turn it off right away. He has to preserve his batteries; they can die, just like that. Who knows how long he'll be here. Without being able to make radio contact, Matt figures he'd better start trying to get out of here on his own. He pushes away some of the rubble and begins to dig with his hands—not sure where it'll lead, but it's got to be somewhere better than where he is now. A lot of stuff he pushes away is soft, mostly dust and soot. He still can't see. It's as if he's a blind miner in a collapsed shaft.

He keeps crawling and digging, coughing and spitting. Someone behind him is doing the same. Finally, the darkness lightens; things are taking shape. He can see that the steel railings of the stairwell have twisted around him. It's like being stuck inside playground monkey bars. *Shit.*

He and two other firefighters, on their bellies, squeeze through to a wider space, just at the precipice of what's left of the building. There's some daylight, though it's not a daylight he's seen before. A veil of soot obscures an angry orange ball in the sky. Minutes ago—or was it hours?—they were 60 feet above the street. Now, they're just 30 feet above a surface, no longer the street. It's a surface of rubble and ruin.

The Marriott is destroyed. All that's left is a sliver of the building. A few lives have been spared because they were at the right place in this sliver.

Matt and two others crawl along the rubble, along the edge, trying to find a way down. The lieutenant and Angel are gone. Mike Mullan, his friend who would soon buy an engagement ring, is gone, too.

Suddenly, desperate voices come from the rubble a few yards away. The firefighters scramble over, and push and pull a pile of debris to the side. Two civilians are under a fallen I-beam. Another couple of inches and they'd be dead. They're out of their minds with fear, but they're okay. Matt wants to ask how the hell they got here, but there's no time for that. They've all got to get out.

They work their way through more dust and rubble, looking for a way down. They're terrified that this remaining portion of the building might collapse as well. On one corner, a huge I-beam is angled down towards the street. They figure it's the only way. Straddling it like a horse, with the civilians between them, the firefighters slide down.

■ Deputy Chief Hayden is alive. He's not sure how or why, but he's alive. The world turns from dark to dim. It's extremely quiet. There are no streets, just mounds of twisted steel and concrete. It's dreamlike, surreal. Survivors walk aimlessly, quietly. People who were there, in the street, moments ago, are gone. He knows some of the top chiefs, his friends—Pete Ganci, Bill Feehan, and Ray Downey—are dead.

Covered in dust and soot, Hayden drifts a bit further south, further into the devastated area. Although the eerie quiet remains, there are frequent emotional outbursts by survivors and those just arriving. There is simultaneous silence and chaos.

■ When the blackness lifts at Stuyvesant High School, Tommy and a handful of others go back outside. Out of the hanging cloud on street level, more firefighters, police, and civilians start to emerge. Guys call out engine and ladder numbers, hoping to find out who's okay and who's missing. Soon, a couple of chiefs are on the scene and they go about trying to organize things.

Besides shock and fear, there's dread in the air because so many radios are malfunctioning or are out altogether. There's simply no way to contact many other firefighters; no way to know who needs help, who's missing, or who's just separated from their regular companies. There's no way to know what, if anything, might happen next.

A Federal Bureau of Investigation (FBI) agent bursts out of the Stuyvesant High School doorway, and yells, "Go, go! *Get out of here!*"

The building is full of explosives and they could go off any second. The dozens of people who've gathered in front of the school tear north away from it. It's at once terrifying and absurd. No one wants to get blown up, but there's something odd about running for your life. Many of the group are in their 40s and 50s and haven't had to run like this in decades, or maybe never, or not since the neighborhood bully and his friends chased them after school. First, it's a morning like any other; now, middle-aged people are running through the streets of Manhattan for dear life.

Tommy steps out of the stampede to yell at a Con Edison worker who's gathering his tools. "Yo, get the fuck out of here! The school's loaded with explosives. Fuck your tools." It seems to register with the Con Ed worker, who leaves his tools and bursts into a sprint.

Tommy, 42, used to be a locomotive on the football field, but now feels like he's never run faster than today. Maybe a thousand feet away, he puts his hands on his knees to catch his breath. Others standing next to him—some who look like they've never run before, much less on a football field—apparently found something inside to dart, dash, or barrel to safety.

Tommy has the urge to say, "We're too old for this shit"—the way someone might say it when they wake up with a hangover, or after pulling a muscle going from home to first in a softball game—but the comment doesn't fit. Too old for this shit? What exactly is the *shit* we're in? Jesus, if they keep running north, they're gonna be in the Bronx.

The crowd keeps its distance; everyone's alert, ready to race away again on any signal. Planes crashing, buildings falling, bombs planted who knows where. There's never a moment when you can breathe that sigh of relief. You can't say you made it, because you don't what might happen next.

Fires are everywhere. Cars, fire engines, and trucks; debris on the street. Buildings near where the towers once stood are on fire. Guys wait their whole careers to fight fires like these; now, no one is even considering them.

After a short while—maybe 15 or 20 minutes—somebody waves for them to come back to Stuyvesant. There's no bomb, no explosives. False alarm. The building will be used as a shelter and triage center.

He starts back . . . slow, wary.

■ Matt and the others stumble towards the river, away from the hell. The sky above them is charcoal gray, but the sun is unmistakably blood red. A small FDNY fireboat pulls to the water's edge. Someone on board asks if they want to ride to an emergency room in a hospital across the river in New Jersey. Matt nods yes.

"Okay, hold on until we tie up and set up a ladder."

There was no holding on at this point. Three of them leap onto the boat. "Get us the fuck out of here, please!"

Matt lay on the deck of the boat as it heads across the Hudson. He's numb. He's not sure what happened. Off the stern, the New York skyline is stolen, gone. The remains of the two towers are splayed like huge hands, gesturing *why*?

He knows his friends are dead. Guys right behind him in the Marriott. Friends who worked in the towers. They're dead. Gone. He wants to cry, get angry, something, but he's just numb—though his pulse suggests otherwise. At the triage area, his pulse remains at 120. A nurse tells him to calm down. He almost laughs hysterically. *Calm down?*

■ It's dust-covered devastation. Another planet. Chief Hayden makes his way to a partially crushed rig. The 54-year-old Hayden pulls himself up on the fire truck, then climbs to the top, overlooking the immediate area and scores of confused, shocked, and scared people. Although generally soft-spoken, Hayden realizes there is a need to pull things together, to establish a presence.

Hundreds look up when he calls their attention. He takes off his helmet. "We lost about 400 guys here today. Let's have a moment of silence for the brothers."

Hayden's gesture and words bring immediate calm and order. The hundreds of firefighters and emergency responders take off their helmets as well and bow their heads for a long time.

Then Hayden put his helmet back on. "Okay. Now we go to work." His voice is strong and sure, carrying the timbre of a football coach. "We've been hit hard, but we gotta regroup. We're gonna pull together right now! We lost a lot of guys and we don't want to lose anymore. We're gonna get organized. You're gonna give your names to chiefs and get your assignments. Step up. Stand tall. We want to save who we can, but we gotta do this the right way. *Let's go!*"

The dust-covered chief atop the rig rallying the troops won't soon be forgotten. There are intermittent shouts of approval and encouragement. People are nodding. The chief's right. There's a job to do.

■ Flip Mullen thinks, Oh great. What a way to die. The guy driving the motorcycle is bouncing along the cobblestone streets near the South Street Seaport. Flip doesn't think he can hang on. He's gonna fall off the bike and die in the gutter with all this fish smell and oil. He sees the firehouse of Ladder 15 ahead, so he just has to hang on a few more seconds. Christ.

Flip gets off the bike, never finding out who the firefighter was—though he finds out later he thinks it's a firefighter they call The Fonz. He steps into something that looks like an oversized junkyard shrouded in dust.

He spots Whipper Stathis and says, "Come on. Let's go this way."

The sight of Flip in his Rescue 1 helmet, carrying a monstrous chain saw he's pulled off a rig, makes Whipper smile just a bit. Wordlessly, they climb a pile of rubble and begin searching for survivors.

▪ As the darkness lifts on West Street, Palmer Doyle and the guys from Engine 254 help free a Port Authority cop who was buried in the rubble. A short while later, he sees a woman covered with debris. He rushes to help her, only to discover she's clearly dead— the debris is not covering her at all because all that remains is her head and upper torso.

▪ After Steve Stathis gets instructions to meet at the Con Ed Emergency Services department at Beekman Downtown Hospital, he barrels through Brooklyn and then into the Battery Tunnel. He has to slam on his brakes as a wall of soot suddenly blackens the road. He's got to inch the car along, using the windshield wipers to brush off clumps of dirt and dust. He finally exits the tunnel—a place where he's been many, many times—but it's as if he went in the tunnel in regular life and came out the other end into some netherworld of dust and pandemonium. Although it's just past noon, everything and everyone is charcoal or slate black. It's lower Manhattan after a midnight snowstorm in an old black-and-white movie. He's pointed to Beekman by a cop layered in soot, and weaves his way through people covered in thick powder, past emergency vehicles with blinking lights barely visible under piles of more dust.

▪ Tommy tries to reach Eileen at work by cell phone, but all he gets is her voice mail. He wants to let her know that he's okay, but he wants to know if she's okay as well. He hears somebody say that terrorists took down the Eiffel Tower. Who knows, something might be blowing up in mid-town. There's no answer at home either. The kids must still be in school.

By early afternoon, Stuyvesant is a mess. Dust on the floor has turned to mud, and workers of all stripes—Emergency Service

Unit, Red Cross, FBI, firefighters, police, and Secret Service—go in and out of the building as they establish their bases of operation. Food is available—stuff that'll get you by, but it's not of the highest nutritional value: candy bars, bug juice, and Dinty Moore stew. The place stinks. People use 5-gallon bottles of Deer Park water to make toilets flush because most are broken, clogged, or overflowing.

A lot of firefighters mingle outside, not sure if they should go a few blocks south to assist in rescue efforts or go over to World Trade Center Seven—a building 47 stories high, which is burning out of control.

Chiefs say to stand down; they want to regroup—no easy feat with nonexistent or sporadic radio communication. There's also the sheer number of firefighters to manage. By the afternoon, thousands have arrived: many in gear, many in street clothes; many on duty, many off duty.

■ Billy and Sean Heeran walk north on the FDR Drive. Numb, helpless, in shock. They're desperate for news about Charlie, and they get some. They see a friend who says he's seen Charlie with another friend. Their first impulse is to celebrate, go get a beer somewhere.

At a mid-town bar, Sean's cell phone rings. "Hey, Sean, it's *Charlie!*"

Sean screams into the phone. *"Where the hell are you?"*

There's a pause. "What are you talking about?"

"Is this Charlie Heeran?"

"No." It's another friend named Charlie, calling to check on Sean.

■ Steve pulls up to Beekman Downtown Hospital and joins the Con Ed emergency crews taking shape. He sees what must be 40 or 50 doctors and nurses waiting at the emergency room entrance with gurneys. Their faces tell the story. It's been hours since the collapse and no victims have arrived.

▪ Chiefs and other officers do what they can to inject order into operations, but there is widespread confusion. Some firefighters are told to get off piles of rubble—it's too dangerous. Some of them say, Fuck you. I'm searching for my men. Huge fires are still going. Trade Center Building Seven looks like it will collapse.

Retired firefighter Flip Mullen sees old friend Chief Pete Hayden on the crushed rig, and tells him he's there to help; Whipper Stathis is there, too. Hayden gives them a quick thanks and instructs them to check in the vicinity of the U.S. Customs building, but not to get too close to Building Seven.

Before going to search, Whipper turns to Hayden, a cell phone in his hand. "You wanna call Rita?"

Hayden smiles. Good idea.

▪ George Johnson and others search nearby buildings, but find them evacuated. There's nothing much else to do but start digging in the pile, hoping to find survivors. It's not long before he hears that a lot of the top brass of the FDNY are dead. After hours of digging, the rumor becomes a fact when one of the top chiefs is found under the rubble. After a long struggle trying to free the body, the men put the chief in a stretcher (called a "stokes basket") and cover him up. Everyone instantly realizes it's a profound moment. They form a long double line, and pass the stretcher down the pile to a cleared area near a command post. Men pray as the body passes them. Some salute; some remark what a great man he was.

After more digging, George is grabbed by an officer to get water for the men. To retrieve water and supplies at a supply stand, George and a couple of other guys traverse a pile of rubble. It's a few seconds before he realizes the red color underfoot is the top side of a fire rig.

At the supply stand, George throws a case of bottled water on his shoulder to bring back to the pile. He doesn't go 50 feet before every bottle is gone, as parched firefighters and rescuers relieve him of every drop. He finds himself repeating this over and over until he finally stations himself high on a steel I-beam to pass out bottles as guys come down from the rubble.

It's not long before Dan McWilliams, another firefighter from his company Ladder 157, asks him to come along. He needs a hand. "Let's hurry before World Trade Center Seven collapses."

■ Tommy calls home again and, this time, the baby-sitter, Patsy, answers. Tommy feels a jolt of emotion, simply because he's connected to home. He says he's fine and that she should just tell the kids the same. Patsy tells him he has to talk to T.J., but he feels too choked up to talk to his 13-year-old son. She repeats, "You *have* to talk to T.J."

As soon as T.J. gets on the phone, he cries. "Daddy, you're not in the buildings?"

Tommy's legs almost give out. He can barely speak. "I'm fine, Teej." He wants to reach through the phone with both arms and hug that kid. He's happy that T.J. is full of talk, excitement, and tears—if he has to talk much, he'll lose it.

■ Flip Mullen, Whipper Stathis and hundreds of others climb and scramble over rubble, searching, but there's little reason to be hopeful. A few injured people are pulled from the debris, which triggers a short buzz of hope, but the air is mostly heavy with dust and a stunned silence, a silence rife with despair.

■ Donnie Howard, one of the captains of Tommy's firehouse, had bolted out of his house in Rockaway, sped to the firehouse for his gear, then to lower Manhattan. The trip that might normally take an hour took Howard 25 minutes.

Howard, Palmer Doyle and hundreds of others now watch helplessly as World Trade Center Seven burns out of control. It's the biggest fire they've ever seen and they're instructed to stand back. It's difficult. People who live to fight fires must stand there and watch the blaze win. A lot of firefighters, however, remain too close—instincts refusing to let them back off completely. When the building finally does start to collapse at 5:20 PM, there is a wild rush for safety.

What would have been a monumental event—the total collapse of a building 47 stories high—seems like a mere firecracker to some who survived the tower collapses seven hours before.

■ Tommy's shift ends at 6 PM and he wants to go home in the worst way. He wants to hug Eileen and the kids and never let them go, but he can't go home yet. He's got to look for missing friends and find out what he can. He's on the first day of three straight day tours, but he'll let some paper pusher worry about manpower. Right now, he knows he'll be here through the night.

He calls home again, and this time gets Eileen. From T.J., the baby-sitter, and various phone messages, she'd known Tommy was all right for a few hours, but he hadn't heard anything about her, so he's relieved to hear her voice.

She and thousands of others had evacuated Manhattan on foot across the 59th Street Bridge hours earlier. On the Queens side, subway service was halted or wildly altered, so the best Eileen could do was to hop a train to Brooklyn.

She took the F Line to the edge of Park Slope and Windsor Terrace, and got out hoping to find a taxi or car service to Rockaway. She headed across the street to use a telephone in Farrell's, a famous Brooklyn watering hole, where Tommy's friend and one of the captains of his firehouse, Vinny Brunton, often tended bar. Not that he'd be there now. He'd certainly be downtown with Tommy.

Before she stepped into Farrell's, she saw a friend, who said he'd give her a ride to Rockaway. In the car, she wished she had called that taxi instead. It was a wild, careening ride through Brooklyn. Her friend, upset by events, was screaming and yelling about terrorists as he swerved past pedestrians and through red lights.

Brunton is one of the guys missing, Tommy says into the phone. One of the big reasons he's got to stay through the night, at least.

Vinny and all the others. She doesn't argue, she just tells him to be careful.

God, it's good to hear her voice. For a while, he thought he'd never hear it again; thought he'd taken his last ride on a fire rig. Now he just wanted to throw her and the kids on his shoulders and escape back in time to somewhere normal—like yesterday.

If he could do that, he wouldn't hear the sound of bodies hitting the ground. Plenty of firefighters and other witnesses had a similar thought: How bad must it be on those upper floors if the alternative is to jump? It's a nightmarish thought, and nightmarish memories remain for witnesses.

One firefighter obsesses about it. Did they die before hitting the ground? Did they die of fright or have heart attacks? Did they close their eyes? Could they hear themselves scream, or were their ears filled with the screaming wind? What were their last thoughts? Did they think about God, or did they have some simple, inexplicable thought? The car needs an oil change. Did the package have enough postage? The people who plunged to the earth had about 15 seconds to have such thoughts. They fell at approximately 100 MPH.

Not all people who hit the ground were jumpers. Not all of them made a choice. Some had tried to lower themselves to safety by climbing down the outside of the tower, only to lose their grip. One man held his jacket open, hoping it might catch the wind as a parachute would. The last-ditch effort actually slowed his descent for a moment, but the wind ripped the jacket out of his hands and he plunged like the others.

Some were pushed. Heat and smoke forced people to the broken windows for air. As they leaned outside, others behind them—also desperate for air—leaned as well, forcing those in front to fall. Still others were essentially propelled into the open air by involuntary reflex.

One firefighter explained it this way. "Put your hand on a hot stove. It will fly off in any direction just to get away from the heat. An entire human body can have a similar reaction. One time, I was trapped in a fire on the third floor and wound up on the garage next door. Somebody told me I was smart to jump. I didn't jump. I just landed there."

■ Chief Hayden can't see much. His corneas have been scratched by the pulverized concrete and steel. He staggers towards an EMS ambulance to get his eyes washed out. Turns out, he's picked a good one—his son, Pete, Jr., who saw the buildings fall and thought the worst—is with the EMS ambulance. Standing there, too, is his brother, Jack, a firefighter. They'd been looking for him all day. His eyes don't work too well, but the tears flow just fine.

It's a great moment, but short. He has to get to a hospital to get some medication for his eyes. After a day of searching and praying, his son and brother don't seem to want to let him leave, so Pete, Jr.—an emergency medical technician with Battalion 4—and Jack ride in the back of the ambulance with the chief to Bellevue Hospital.

■ Billy and Sean Heeran stay at Sean's apartment. They're going to hang on to any thread of hope they can, but they both know the likely, unbearable outcome: Charlie didn't make it.

■ Matt Tansey and others, who'd been taken to New Jersey for treatment, are dropped off by bus at a firehouse in Brooklyn. He's wearing hospital scrubs and holding his bunker gear, when his parents arrive to drive him home to Rockaway.

CHAPTER 4

Everybody's Got a Number

By 1907, Belle Harbor had enough year-round residents to support a Catholic parish. The cornerstone for St. Francis de Sales Church was laid in May. Just two months later, Sunday mass was said before hundreds of congregants in a new, wooden-steepled structure.

As the number of parishioners continued to climb, church leaders saw the need for a school. By the fall of 1913, St. Francis de Sales School, adjacent to the church, was accepting local children into its grade school. From that point forward, the Beach 129th Street church and school were the de facto community center, though its role was interrupted by a destructive blaze.

On a Friday afternoon in April 1935, the church was empty except for a scattered handful of afternoon worshippers. A woman, kneeling on a side pew, noticed bright orange flames in the front of the church, high above the altar. Her shock and fear echoed through the church. She and the others ran outside, and alerted men on the street and priests in the nearby rectory.

As the fire raged above them in the ceiling, men and priests dodged falling embers and grabbed what valuables they could. The priests cleared the altar, then hurried to the side aisles and grabbed carved Stations of the Cross from the walls. The men joined together and hauled a 10-foot wooden statue of St. Francis de Sales—the patron saint of writers, journalists, and teachers—out of the burning building just as Engine 268 and other companies were arriving.

Eventually, more than 250 firefighters joined Engine 268 to fight the fire. Some of the firefighters ran hose lines through the brick school building next door, sending water through windows onto the second floor of the church. However, St. Francis de Sales Church, made of pine and oak, was soon devoured by the fire. Hundreds of people had gathered to watch, and now they stayed until nothing was left except a charred skeletal structure. The rectory and convent were spared as a steady wind steered the fire away from them towards vacant lots.

Two days later, six masses were held in the nearby auditorium. The cause of the fire remained unknown, though painters using blowtorches were suspected of leaving behind smoldering sparks that, at some point, broke into flames. Father John Patterson, the pastor, said a drive for a new brick church would soon commence. In the near future, he told the congregation, tents would be erected on an adjacent lot to accommodate the large summer crowds that would soon be attending Sunday mass.

Parishioners made the campaign for a new church a quick success. Two years later, a new, brick, virtually fireproof church welcomed the community by the beach.

September 2001

In Rockaway, after the Twin Towers collapse and as soon as it appears the attacks have ended, a peninsula-wide desperate attempt to account for firefighters and people who worked "downtown" begins. Things are particularly feverish in the west end neighborhoods where many of those firefighters live. Rumors become the new roller coaster of Rockaway. Good news followed by bad, followed by good, followed by worse.

Danny Suhr, the burly man, busy with a pizza business on the side and just getting used to his new home in Rockaway, is confirmed dead—the first firefighter to die on September 11. He was killed by the force of a jumper from one of the top floors of the World Trade Center. The beloved priest, Father Mychal Judge, was hit administering last rites to Danny.

All the guys in Ladder 105 are missing. Tommy Carroll's with them, right? Poor, unlucky bastard. No, he got detailed to Engine

226. Engine 226? They're missing at least three. No, he never took that detail. He wound up going with 210. He's okay.

Has anybody heard anything about Kevin Lunny? His wife, Pat, isn't home and the house is dark.

An e-mail circulates: Jimmy Morgan, a captain on the fire department for just a couple of days, is dead. John Moran, the battalion chief with two young kids at home, was inside the buildings.

Anybody hear anything about other firefighters? How about Harry Werner? Sean Reen? Any word on Eddie Cashen or Billy Collins? Mike Lee or Brian Davan or Gerry Davan? Jeez, there are so many.

Kenny Whelan, captain of the firehouse on Beach 116th Street, is trying to get news of missing firefighters as well. Although he'd been on vacation, he jumped in his car and raced back to the firehouse as soon as he saw the buildings collapse on television. He didn't know there had been a "total recall" of all active firefighters. He, like many others, just responded. Now, he's dispensing information when he gets it and awaits a rescue and recovery assignment.

Bernie Heeran hears that Charlie might've somehow gotten out, though he knows helicopters were never used to rescue people from the roof of the Twin Towers. Charlie's probably in one of the hospitals. Some victims ended up in New Jersey hospitals, so you had better check there. Like Matt Tansey—he called home from the Jersey Medical Center.

Hope and unreliable information runs unbridled on the grapevine. A trauma center in Brooklyn gets a phone call: Get ready. They've found an air pocket or void with 300 to 400 survivors.

More good news. Jimmy Morgan is not dead. Sully talked to his sister. He's definitely okay. The new captain had been sent to the Bronx that morning.

The trauma center gets another call an hour later: Sorry, the report was a mistake. No air pocket was found; no survivors on the way.

Palmer Doyle? He's okay. Eddie Greene? He's okay. His eyes are all screwed up, but he's okay.

Richie Allen? He's just a Probie. He can't be missing.

Steve Belson? What about him? Firefighter, lifeguard, surfer—the Jewish guy, big handlebar mustache, the guy called Bells or O'Belson? Missing, someone said. Same with Eugene Whelan. Ah man, he lives in an apartment above the Harbor Light.

Anybody hear anything about Farmer? It's not easy to get news on him because Farmer is a nickname. His given name is Tom McCann and there's a Tom McCann missing, presumed dead. Maybe it's not the Tom McCann from down here, from Rockaway. No one knows for sure.

Mike Andrews is dead. He worked for Cantor Fitzgerald, just like Charlie Heeran. Mike's 10 years older, but they're both Xavier guys. In the early 1980s, Mike was part of a trend of Rockaway kids who headed into the city to Xavier High School on West 16th Street.

Rockaway doesn't have a parochial high school, so kids educated at St. Francis and other local schools often head to other parts of Queens or Manhattan for high school. The kids who choose Xavier—a Jesuit school that can count Supreme Court Justice Antonin Scalia and Pulitzer Prize winner Dave Anderson among its graduates—accept the daily, long haul into Manhattan. The ride on the subway is a good hour and one-half each way, but the commute seems like a small sacrifice.

It's a privilege to be accepted into the all-boys school. It deserves its stellar academic reputation. Although the academics program is a draw, a big part of the appeal is word-of-mouth stuff you hear from guys like Mike Andrews. They'd come back to the neighborhood boasting about the school. The books weren't easy, but it was worth it. They'd say it was great to be on the basketball or football teams, but rugby was even better. The rugby team went to places like Ireland, France, Puerto Rico, and Utah.

The word caught on. Going into Manhattan seemed grown-up enough; these Xavier kids were seeing the world, too. Parents with grade-school kids started to hear how Xavier students were getting into good colleges and then getting good jobs on Wall Street. The pipeline between Rockaway and Xavier was up and running. If kids were going to choose between firefighting and finance, Xavier was clearly a good stepping stone for the life in a suit and tie. The word got out: Xavier alumni help you out when they can. Not that you'd be shunning one life for another by going to Xavier. Plenty of Rockaway kids go to Xavier, then to college, and then to the fire department.

Now, it's more popular than ever. A dozen kids from Rockaway will start freshman year at Xavier in the fall of 2002, joining dozens of Rockaway kids already in attendance. More than a dozen wanted to attend, but gaining admission has become more competitive. Each year, the Egan family hosts an "open house" at their home on Rockaway Beach Boulevard for prospective students. They make it clear that a great tradition, network, and support system is in place for Rockaway kids who choose Xavier.

The message the Egans convey is that Xavier is like family. Counting current students and graduates, there are hundreds of Xavier families in Rockaway. When news circulates that former Xavier students are missing, Rockaway has reason to take it hard. It's family, after all. Maybe not related by blood, but it is family.

Matt Burke—younger than Mike Andrews, older than Charlie Heeran—is also missing. A stockbroker now, he was once a star quarterback at Xavier. His father is the assistant headmaster at the school. And everyone knows Jimmy Riches. He spent summers in Rockaway, played ball in the summer league. He graduated from Xavier in '89. He's one of the missing firefighters.

Those firefighters are about family, too. Firefighters eat together and share sleeping quarters. They have to use extraordinary teamwork to do their jobs. They call each other "brother."

Rockaway is often called a close-knit community. It's clear why: the ties are familial or something near to that. Chances are that somebody on the block is a firefighter; either he's missing or you feel for him because you know he's lost "brothers," maybe a lot of brothers. Or somebody else has ties to Xavier. Either that person is missing or someone's classmate is. You might be lucky if you're once-removed—friends of friends might be missing or dead—but, in Rockaway, that's about as removed as you'll get. After all, almost 500 firefighters live on the peninsula. Many others from Rockaway work at the World Trade Center. You're going to know someone.

Like everywhere, people in Rockaway are glued to their television sets. Watching TV for disaster news is an old habit. The images are not that different from disaster movies, Oklahoma City, or the space shuttle *Challenger,* and too many floods and earthquakes to recall. Of course, this is different. The country has been attacked—not just New York—and the buildings collapse on live TV. When the buildings fall and the tape is played repeatedly, you ask, how many dead? Reporters tell us that, between workers and visitors, as many as 140,000 people are in the World Trade Center each day. So how many are dead? Five, ten, twenty thousand? It's immediately clear how different this feels from other "TV" events. Locals—true in any disaster—must ask themselves, do I know someone?

If you live outside New York, it's a terrible, horrifying, and numbing event. In New York, in Rockaway, it's desperate. *This is about your family.*

■ Although Tommy's been told to stand down, he gets stir crazy at Stuyvesant and heads south towards evening. Maybe it's his years working construction giving him the perspective, but he immediately senses that rescue efforts won't reap much reward.

Maybe the voids or air pockets will prove havens for some, but Tommy looks at the dust and thinks the worst. That dust is concrete and steel. Humans don't have a chance. He sees the crushed rig of 105. He's got a radio and uses it frequently—"210 to 105"— but never gets an answer. He's already heard that hospitals, ready for an unprecedented flood of victims, remain quiet.

■ There's an urge to go out, to see who you might see. Maybe you'll see someone you really don't know, but if you happen to see them, it'll answer the question. They made it. Others can't watch the television—they've got to get to church. The bells are ringing. It's an unusual sound in Belle Harbor. The clock, its face on the church steeple, has chimed at appointed hours, but the bells have gone unused for long stretches of time.

Monsignor Geraghty remembers Billy Egan saying something months earlier about how the church bells used to ring when he was growing up, and Marie Farragher telling him that the church bells rang on VE Day—the victory in Europe on May 8, 1945. Geraghty rings the bells, grateful for the community memory he was given, and then gets ready for a 7:30 PM mass.

He is expecting a handful of people and is soon surprised to see scores of congregants fill the pews of the church that holds 600 people. Before mass, Geraghty addresses the crowd, letting them know that prayers will be offered for those missing or killed earlier in the day. Someone calls out a name and asks for others to pray. Then someone else calls out another name and then someone else another. The names are offered tentatively at first: Agnello, Moran, Allen, Mulligan, King. Palazzo, Morgenstern, Sullivan, Russell.

Voices—some cracking, some defiant—call out more names in quicker fashion. Slavin. O'Rourke. Heeran. Farrell. Pfeifer. The list is at once heart-wrenching and eye-opening. There will be many dead. That much Geraghty and everyone already know from seeing things on television. Yet now, hearing the names echo in the church—Suhr, Dewan, Gregory, Peterson, Riches, Heffernan, Andrews, Munson—it's clear that many from Rockaway will be among the dead.

There's good news as well. People come into church to report the names of people who were unaccounted for, but have since arrived home safely. Somebody runs into church, where now hundreds have gathered, and says excitedly, "They just found firefighter Walter Hynes—he's alive!" The church explodes in cheers. Ronnie, his wife, is sitting there by the baptistery. She's clearly elated.

Geraghty senses something, maybe a firefighter or someone in the know, shaking their heads. The report on Walter Hynes is unconfirmed. Everyone wants to have hope, but they don't want it to hang on a false report.

■ For Tommy, it's a night of back and forth. He goes back to Stuyvesant where he's supposed to get some sleep, then back to the site because sleep won't come. He feels helpless at the scene. There's a buzz of confusion. Is heavy equipment going to be moved in to start moving some of the massive debris? It doesn't seem so because rescue teams are arriving—some are guys who specialize in finding people in caves. Teams of rescue dogs are being lined up to do searches.

He goes back to Stuyvesant. Never quite able to get all the crap out of his eyes, he takes a seat and allows a nurse to spray water into his eyes. The improved vision also affords him a small laugh. Sitting next to him, waiting to have his eyes washed, is a German shepherd—a search and rescue dog. He half expects the dog to say something like, "Tough day, huh?"

He lays down on one of the cots they've set up, then sits up. It's a job of inches. He's heard by now that a jumper killed Danny Suhr. He had just seen him in Rockaway. Another couple of inches and maybe Danny would've made it, or another firefighter would've been killed. Some made right turns and lived; some made left turns and died. Same thing with scheduling, the details and mutuals. Scheduling either saved you or got you killed. You never know. He thought about all those times he cursed his bad luck.

Not anymore.

■ Firefighters, cops, and others are told to stop digging. The work is too dangerous because adequate lighting has not yet been installed. Some grumble or plead, a few more minutes, chief, but soon it's a real order. *Stop.*

A handful of firefighters staggering along see the doors open to a Mexican restaurant. One turns towards the place, then another. Soon the five or six are at the bar with cold beers. They are thirsty and need a drink. In 10 minute's time, there are 30 firefighters having beers.

Some are crying. Guys hug each other when they see someone for the first time that day. You didn't know who was alive or dead. A familiar face is a beautiful thing. One guy gargles his beer, his dried out throat not yet ready. He spits the mouthful to the floor, then takes a big swallow.

A chief steps inside and stands there. A look of disbelief forms on his face. A couple of firefighters see him, then turn back to the bar.

"What the fuck is the matter with you guys?" All heads turn. One firefighter—a big guy no one messes with—looks ready to tear the chief in two. "I've been standing here a good 30 seconds and nobody's offered me a fuckin' beer."

The big firefighter steps towards him and throws his arm around the chief. "Get the man a beer!"

Some guys toss dollar bills on the bar before leaving.

▪ Men like Whipper Stathis, Flip Mullen, and hundreds of others head home well past midnight. They'll be back in a few hours. Flip stands for a moment at the mouth of the Battery Tunnel. A Port Authority cop asks if he'd like a ride. Flip says he's going to Rockaway.

"Hop in!"

▪ By the next morning, word gets out that it was a false report. The news delivered in church about firefighter Walter Hynes being in a hospital was wrong. Walter, husband to Ronnie and father of three daughters, is dead.

Not everyone knew he was also an attorney. It was the kind of morsel you'd pick up about the missing and the dead that pierced you, made you realize how much was taken that day. Nobody was "just" a firefighter or "just" a bond trader or office worker. Wally Hynes was a captain on the fire department *and* a lawyer. That means he took the lieutenant test, the captain test, and all those law exams—a lot of studying while still fighting fires and saving lives—*and* he played the bagpipes, *and* he was there plenty of days to meet his girls getting out of school. Rockaway people knew more than a firefighter was gone—a great guy was gone.

The world is going to hear about the numbers lost. Will they hear about the people lost? Within a minute's time, you'd see others' lives with greater appreciation, but there's hardly any time to think at all. You still haven't heard anything about Joe McCormack and Danny Marzano? How about the McDades? Kevin Callaghan? Brian Becker? Kevin Dowdell? He was with Rescue 4, right? It doesn't look good.

Timmy Stackpole, a new captain, was supposed to finish up at Engine 219 that morning, then head over to division headquarters. He was the guy who came back to the job after being so badly burned when a floor collapsed in a Brooklyn fire just a few years before. He survived that but didn't survive this one. No surprise to hear that he headed into the city instead of going to division when he heard what was going on at the Trade Center.

Pete Frontera was seen and so were the Featherstons, husband and wife, Pat and Bethanne. There are so many. Who are you forgetting? Oakie O'Connor. Pat Savage. Peter Brady. Eddie Mullen. Kevin Redden. You list names, hoping somebody knows something, but soon enough, the rumors slow and hopes fade as surviving firefighters, witnesses to the horror, return to the neighborhood. They deliver sobering news. There's no one to save.

▪ What do they mean? One building, then the other, fell on Petey Hayden. He walked away. He came out covered in dust, barking orders to all the firefighters. He survived, didn't he? Anything's possible. There's still hope.

You gotta have hope. Word just came in: Joe Farrell's okay. So is John Donovan. Hey, what about Mike Sullivan? Isn't he retired? That doesn't mean anything. Guys like Flip Mullen, out of the job for years, shot right in there. Somebody says they saw Mike Basmagy.

Some guys you just know by their first name, so it's nearly impossible to be sure of the news you get when the name is Kevin. There are so many: Kevin Lunny, Kevin Judge, Kevin Dolan, Kevin McCabe, Kevin Redden, Kevin Dowdell, Kevin Callaghan, Kevin O'Rourke.

John Moran is dead. A battalion chief. Like Wally Hynes, a lawyer. Damn, somebody says, he used to play bass in a band that used to play Rockaway bars. His brother Mike is okay. Oakie O'Connor and Jimmy Cashin were seen right here in Rockaway. It's good to have eyewitnesses. Yeah, but Joe Agnello is missing. John Heffernan, too.

■ You get information on the grapevine, at the stores, or in church. Unless you're family or a very close friend, you don't want to call the house of someone who might be missing. What if they tell you so-and-so is dead? What if they ask why you're calling? To satisfy a morbid curiosity? You don't want to tie up the telephone lines either. Maybe the family is waiting by the phone for news.

That story about a man who lived by "riding the building down" or "riding the rubble" is just that—a story. A story just as false but less cruel than the one perpetrated by a woman who said she had received a phone call from her husband who was buried under the ruins. She said he was a Port Authority police officer trapped in the rubble with 10 other officers. (Months later, Sugeil Mejia, 24, would be sentenced to three years in prison for the hoax.)

Someone else says they saw Bob Johnson, and Bob's brother, George Johnson, is definitely okay. Check out the newspaper. That's a Rockaway boy! He's one of the three guys in that picture raising the American flag!

■ After not sleeping at Stuyvesant, but having regular nightmares, Tommy and a buddy head down to the site. They're sent to the New York Marriott Hotel—another hotel in the chain, which is two blocks south of the collapsed Marriott of the World Trade

Center—and relieve a crew that had a "watch line" set up through a window. A watch line is a charged line or hose remaining at the scene of a fire with a detail of firefighters to guard against possible rekindling after the fire has apparently been extinguished. In other words, you "watch" to make sure the fire doesn't kick up again.

Tommy's not in the Marriott very long before he's relieved. It's another indication that there are probably too many people who want to help. Thousands of firefighters and rescuers, all keen to chip in, are often getting in each other's way, or feeling helpless while they wait for orders that may or may not ever come. By the time some get to the place the media are already calling "Ground Zero"—a term coined at the dawn of the nuclear age, meaning the area directly under an exploding atomic device—they have already spent hours at staging areas in Brooklyn or elsewhere waiting for a ride to the site. They arrive frustrated and overeager. It's difficult for everyone.

Tommy wishes Ray Downey were here. Chief Ray Downey of Rescue Operations (of the Special Operations Command) is missed. A world-renowned expert in search and rescue, Downey had addressed the U.S. Congress in 1998 on first responder duties and capabilities in the event of a terrorist attack involving weapons of mass destruction. Three years prior to his appearance before Congress, Downey helped save lives in Oklahoma City when he evaluated the tottering and bombed Murrah Building with a skillful eye, and worked with teams to shore up the structure so rescue and recovery operations could proceed. Like Peter Ganci, he was always a hands-on type. In Oklahoma City, he worked with local firefighters and FEMA (Federal Emergency Management Agency) teams to place support beams that prevented the rubble from shifting.

Perhaps Downey would have suggested getting cranes in immediately to remove massive I-beams before starting with hand digging and bucket brigades. Perhaps not, but he'd probably be the one making the call. The often-overlooked aspect of the September 11 attacks is the talent and experience that was stolen forever. With some of the best guys gone, there's a lot of seat-of-the-pants, learn-as-you-go management. Some of the reason there are so few available, capable replacements is because the city—with the fire commissioner's capitulation—had cut back on senior staff chiefs. Had it had a full complement of staff chiefs, some key personnel would have been trained and could have stepped in to the void left by Ganci, Downey, and Feehan.

There's smoke and dust in the air, but the plain truth is evident in the open space: the Twin Towers are gone. The two massive structures of the World Trade Center were 1,368 feet tall and climbed 110 stories. From street level, huge buildings—50 and 60 stories high—still loom over the area. Now that the towers are gone, it's difficult to imagine how a man-made structure could actually be twice the size of these remaining, mostly nameless behemoths.

Each floor, in each tower, was approximately 210 feet square. In other words, each floor held approximately an acre of rentable floor space, giving the Twin Towers a combined 220 acres of space, approximately 9 million square feet. It is estimated that 10% of the office space in Manhattan was lost on September 11.

It's a matter of perspective. There's a gaping hole in the skyline, yet the wreckage stands seven stories high. Seven stories are 70 to 80 feet in the air—a big pile, for sure. Yet, that also means 110 stories were condensed into seven . . . 1,368 feet flattened into 70 or 80.

It's not surprising to hear people say the explosions sounded like bombs. A large tractor-trailer rig hauling gasoline, like those you see transporting gasoline on interstate highways or refilling the underground tanks at a gas station, carries approximately 10,000 gallons of gasoline. The Boeing 767s that crashed into the towers each carried 24,000 gallons—nearly 2.5 times the amount of a fuel truck. The planes weighed approximately 400,000 pounds.

While working in the lobby of the north tower, Chief Hayden considered the possibility of a collapse early on, but he knew distress calls from the top floors were flooding emergency lines. He and others had to weigh how much of a collapse it would be. The whole building couldn't collapse, could it? How long would it take firefighters to get to the top floors, make rescues, and get out? It was just one hour and two minutes after the second plane hit that the south tower collapsed

To many people watching from a distance or on television, and even to observers on the scene, the towers looked as though they would remain standing. While the plane crashes had taken huge chunks out of both towers, the overall structures seemed to be intact. A few experts, after the fact, said they knew total collapse was inevitable and imminent because the towers, designed differently from the Empire State Building and other skyscrapers, used exterior walls as load-bearing walls. The design allowed for open space on office floors, but eased the way for the building to pancake or fall in on itself.

It's one of the primary reasons the towers did not tip over like trees on the end of a lumberjack's axe. Whereas a tree is solid, the buildings were mostly air or empty space; there is no solid stump underneath to force it to the side. If it had a stump, it was the 70 feet of foundation *below* ground. The design, combined with gravity and momentum, ensured the buildings could only collapse upon themselves.

Some feared the worst right away because the towers had more steel than concrete—another break from traditional skyscraper construction. The design proved more than adequate when the buildings faced hurricane-strength winds on numerous occasions—it was designed to withstand winds of 140 MPH—and when the terrorist truck bomb was set off in the basement nine years earlier.

However, as any firefighter can tell you, the more concrete, the more fire resistance. Although a collapse could probably happen with any skyscraper (given the elements of high impact and jet fuel), the better the fire resistance, the more time for evacuation.

When the planes hit the two towers, the collisions damaged the structures in two major ways. First, they knocked out a large number of vertical support columns. In both buildings, columns around the edge or outer walls were damaged. In the north tower, those columns—and vertical columns at the building's core—were knocked out. Second, the collisions also ignited the planes' fuel supplies, causing a massive explosion that set each building on fire. These fires were also huge and distributed throughout the floors. In many instances, fires will start and spread, but the point of origin will burn itself out and begin to cool. In this case, there wasn't one single point of origin but many. Cooling couldn't happen.

The crash did not take out enough columns to immediately break apart the sturdy steel framework; the remaining columns were strong enough to hold up the top portion of each building. Yet, the severely intense fire heated these standing columns to extremely high temperatures, twisting and weakening them.

In the World Trade Center towers, the support structure was designed to withstand a typical building fire for a few hours or more, to give rescue workers time to evacuate the occupants and possibly extinguish the fire. Such a fire might burn at 800° F as desks, paper, carpets, drapes, and the like are consumed. Such a fire won't melt steel.

A fire of 1,000° F will start to weaken structural steel. The ocean of jet fuel that poured itself on the towers triggered fires that reached temperatures somewhere between 1,500 and 2,000° F. Again, the fire was widespread and enormous, therefore no cooling could occur. Without cooling, the steel couldn't retain its strength.

As key structural elements melted—hastened because the insulation on the steel beams was knocked off or torn away—more of the columns buckled. Without adequate column support at the crash site, the top part of each building collapsed onto the lower part of the building. There were some 20 stories above the areas of impact. Essentially, when the columns collapsed, it was like dropping a 20-story building on top of another building. The forces created by the falling floors on the floors below were far greater than the resistance of these floors, leading to a complete, downward domino or pancake collapse.

Although the south tower was hit second, it was the first to collapse. This occurred because the point of impact was lower on the building, meaning the support columns had a greater load pressing down on them. The greater load caused the buckling to occur sooner.

The huge, gray dust clouds that covered lower Manhattan after the collapse were formed when the concrete floors were pulverized in the fall and then blasted the surrounding neighborhood.

On one hand, there's a resistance to second-guess how things were handled at Ground Zero. After all, there's only so much to prepare for if 19 men pick a random day for a suicide mission. However, second-guessing is an essential step in building a foundation for better, improved firefighting and rescue techniques. Years ago, Monday morning quarterbacking brought forth improvements such as fire walls, stricter building codes, and adequate pumping systems. What will come as a result of September 11 remains to be seen. Fireproofing materials and high-rise building design and codes are among topics sure to be addressed. There will also be the issue of whether to send firefighters in at all.

As the towers burned, collapse was considered, but the consensus was that, if it occurred, it would be a partial collapse and would happen after several hours. The immediate focus was getting people out as fast as possible. Supervisors set up command centers in both lobbies and sent scores of men—many of them high-rise fire specialists—to fight the fire as well as they could and oversee an orderly evacuation. Thousands did get out safely, but the toll on the department was devastating when the buildings imploded.

That undeniable fact will affect future decisions should something similar happen again. Many chiefs have said that they doubt they could ever again send that many firefighters into a building that is essentially under attack. Instead, they would focus on evacuating the area around the building and assess the safety of the structure before trying to rescue people inside.

The commanders at the scene will consider new calculations when measuring the risks to firefighters against the number of lives that can be saved. It takes approximately one minute to clear a floor. How many floors are there? Will people be able to get out from top floors before collapse occurs? The memory of two 110-story buildings pancaking—and how 343 firefighters were killed—will certainly factor into any decision about how to proceed with rescue operations.

Nationwide, roughly 100 firefighters die each year in the line of duty. About half the firefighter fatalities occur at the scene of a fire. Many die of heart attacks; some die in motor vehicle accidents in which the firefighter is struck by a vehicle or while riding in one involved in a crash. Some deaths occur during training; some at nonfire emergencies.

On September 11, 2001, more than three times that number died on a single day on a single job.

■ Tommy is among a thousand people—firefighters, cops, ironworkers, Red Cross, you name it—even celebrities. It's a couple of days later; a warm, Indian summer afternoon in Battery Park City, the section of downtown that lies alongside the Hudson River and is across the street from where the towers stood. Many here are exhausted, their nerves shot.

Out of nowhere, someone yells, "Run!" A mass of people stampede towards the water, dust kicking up. Tommy doesn't know if a building is falling, or if terrorists are shooting at people. He'll ask questions later. One guy doesn't stop running at all. He leaps onto a boat docked at the small marina and falls hard, probably breaking an arm or wrist. A couple of others dive into the water. Some people on the boats hurry to untie the ropes mooring them to the dock. They're getting out of here.

It's a false alarm. Apparently, it was something like the old game of telephone. Someone says something to one person who repeats it to another, but, somewhere along the line, the message gets misconstrued. "That might fall unless it's supported" could easily have been interpreted as "It's going to fall." Throw in some exhaustion and a bad case of nerves, and someone will make the next interpretation: *"Run!"*

A young firefighter, hands on his knees, says to Tommy. "Shit, you're fast! You could play for the Giants. You almost took out Donald Trump."

Tommy doesn't know what he's talking about. Another guy nods his head—he saw that, too. "Too bad you didn't. What the fuck is *he* doing here? Speculating on real estate?"

■ After grabbing a few hours of sleep, Flip Mullen is dropped off at the Flatbush Avenue entrance of the Belt Parkway and stands there in his old FDNY helmet. The first car heading into the city stops and gives him a ride into lower Manhattan. He joins thousands of others there to help. Many are on bucket brigades; some are crawling into voids. After hours of digging in the hot sun, he goes to a makeshift refreshment stand for a cool drink. At the end of a long table, he sees something. Jesus Christ, look at that. It's his old FDNY canvas turnout coat, just hanging there, waiting for him.

■ Palmer Doyle returns to dig. The first three days, he's bouncing on his toes, ready, excited, because today's the day he is going to find survivors. By the fourth and fifth day, he goes to work, his shoulders sagging just a bit.

■ Chief Hayden knew from the start that finding survivors was unlikely. There was just too much devastation. Still, he holds hope as he helps lead a task force of some 1,200 firefighters, formed to oversee rescue and recovery operations.

■ In Rockaway, there is talk of funerals and memorials. For some of the missing, nothing is planned. There exists the excruciating thread of hope to which some people cling. One hundred and ten stories of concrete and steel have been compressed to seven stories of rubble. Hundreds and hundreds of people have likely been cremated, but hope lives, however desperate. Those who waved good-bye to their loved ones who went on the four doomed planes at least know beyond reasonable doubt. Those who waved good-bye to their loved ones leaving for work have hope. That's why so many of them hold photos for the television cameras. They hope that someone has seen their daughter, husband, son.

■ It must've been adrenaline and numbness that got Matt Tansey from the collapsed towers to the boat that took him to the medical center in New Jersey, because now he can't move. It's nearly a week since he was thrown down the stairs, and then spun in a whirlwind of steel and concrete. Still, he needs help getting out of bed.

He'd seen an orthopedic surgeon who saw the swelling and wondered how it was that he hadn't broken his back. It wasn't broken, but something was wrong with it. Then there was his neck. He has suffered a herniated disk in his neck, too. He's 27 and feels like 90. Every step he took that day turned out to be the right step, but he's hurt, his friends are gone, and it's hard to feel lucky.

Logic and evidence say there'll be no survivors, but then there's news of a pharmacy, a jewelry store, and some other stores left virtually intact, just one level below ground. Found by subterranean explorers and rescuers, the mall is frozen in time. Clocks are stopped. Items are set at the cash register. Some stores look as if they can open for business.

Although remarkable because of the extent to which it's been preserved, the mall is a reminder to some that others, besides heroes, were here. Looting occurred. Thousands came to Ground Zero to help, to look for friends and family. Some, dressed in the uniforms of heroes, came to steal from a grave.

Still, it's a scene of hope for some. Maybe survivors have found another spot, equally well preserved. They just can't communicate, but they're in there somewhere. Cell phone and beepers haven't worked since the collapse. Maybe they're in a store with water and Gatorade and things like that. Somebody on the TV just said people have been known to survive for 26 days, as long as they get a little bit of water. It rained on Friday, September 14—maybe that's all the water they'll need to hang in there.

Such hope refuses to wilt in some houses in Rockaway. Yellow ribbons appear on trees and doors.

Difficult as it is, many accept the brutal truth. The oft-overlooked peninsula at the end of Queens has suffered more September 11 losses than any other community. They're saying it could be as many as 90 people. At the Harbor Light, a man at the bar looks over each shoulder, making certain Bernie Heeran isn't around.

"These people didn't just die in some horrible accident. They were killed. *Murdered.*"

Others nod their heads in agreement. "It'll never be the same. When was the last time a place like this, a small town, had so many people murdered?"

CHAPTER 5

Sorrow on the Sand

December 1966

It was exactly three weeks before Christmas and a sad day for the Daly family. They had just buried Gertrude's mother on Long Island and were heading back to Belle Harbor. Gertrude sat in the car beside her husband, James. The four kids were in the back seat. With no warning, James felt his chest start to twist into a knot. He pulled the car to the side of the road, had a heart attack, and died.

The 1966 Christmas season in the Daly's apartment would've been difficult under normal circumstances. It turned catastrophic when fire erupted early Christmas morning.

The Dalys, now just Gertrude and the four kids, lived in one of the four apartments above a couple of stores on Beach 129th Street in Belle Harbor. A snowstorm was in full swing. Next door, Droesch's Bar—sometimes called the Belle Harbor Taverns—still held a handful of customers who'd stopped for a Christmas toast after attending midnight mass at St. Francis on the next block.

The front window looked like a snow globe as flakes fell, lit up by soft streetlights. Every few minutes someone said something about how unusual, how wonderful it was to get a white Christmas. That would make someone think they were Bing Crosby and they'd croon out the old Christmas classic. No one seemed to care that it was just 9° F outside; in the bar, it was warm, cozy, and full of holiday cheer.

The music and merrymaking was interrupted when the door crashed open.

"Fire!"

The first alarm sounded at 2:50 AM. Before Engine 268 on Beach 116th Street arrived, one of the men who lived in the burning building, Frank Blackburn, alerted his neighbors by banging on doors to wake them.

Twelve-year-old Kenny Whelan and his family were led to safety. Blackburn's family got out and so did the Griffins. The Dalys were still inside. Four or five men tried to enter but were turned back by the black smoke. Someone tried scaling the front of the frame building to make a rescue from the second floor but was repelled by fire.

Trucks and engines from Beach 116th Street raced their way to the scene in deep snow and ice. The firefighters attacked the fire in the savage cold. An hour later, firefighters with sheets of ice layered on their backs, moved slowly past the doleful crowd.

Three Daly children were dead; Gertrude and the oldest girl, Bonnie, survived.

Eighteen people were homeless that Christmas morning. Some of the survivors spent the next few nights at the Newport Inn, later to be known as the Harbor Light.

It was a devastating event. George Droesch, the bar owner, collected hundreds of dollars in donations, but it was little solace. Just three weeks earlier, the family had lost its grandmother and father. Now, on Christmas—of all days—three kids were killed.

More than three decades later, it remains an excruciating memory. Talk to anyone who was there and eyes well up, heads shake . . . it was bad.

Autumn 2001

Fort Tilden, the mostly overlooked sanctuary of the peninsula, hosts a candlelight vigil in late September to remember those who were killed less than two weeks before. Three thousand people attend, including Mayor Rudolph Giuliani. He would later tell people in Rockaway that he'd been exhausted and that he almost didn't come. He'd been recovering from treatment for prostate cancer and was utterly drained by the events of the last 12 days.

Rockaway, he said, gave him a second wind, the inspiration to keep going. He tells a handful of people who've expressed their gratitude for his appearance at the vigil, "If you can do it, the least I can do is come here."

Echoing the words of Mayor Hylan nearly 80 years before, Giuliani soon urges a citywide return to normalcy. Go back to work, spend money; the life of the city goes on. In Rockaway, that's not so easy. This is a place where outdoor speakers have to be installed in St. Francis because hundreds of people can't get in the church that's jammed with mourners every few days. Perhaps there'll be a return to normalcy, but not until some time after thousands attend the memorial they'll be holding for Steve Belson at Beach Channel High School.

Or, perhaps, normalcy will return when the surfers do. You walk down to the beach and see the USS *John F. Kennedy* aircraft carrier. It's easy to see why they call it The Big John. It's more than 1,000 feet long and 23 stories from keel to mast top. The area of its flight deck is almost 5 acres. It's a big ocean, but with Long Island on one side and New Jersey on the other, the *John F. Kennedy* looks too big for the tub. It's a clear, massive reminder that things are anything *but* normal. Normalcy won't necessarily return when the carrier steams away.

Normalcy might return when Ladder Truck 137 isn't such a familiar sight at the intersection of Beach 129th Street and Rockaway Beach Boulevard. That's where the rig is stationed during funerals at St. Francis, its aerial ladder raised to a 45° angle, a large American flag hanging from its top rungs.

Normalcy might return if the workers ever stop coughing. As many as 4,000 responders have the "WTC (World Trade Center) cough." Many worked without respirators or used useless paper masks bought in hardware stores, and their lungs were beaten up by air filled with pulverized concrete, glass, and other airborne contaminants.

Normalcy might return if the haunting wail of bagpipes ever subsides.

Normalcy, of course, can't return because things will never be the same . . . certainly not for the Heerans or Charlie's friends.

Rumors compelled Bernie Heeran and his family to search for Charlie in area hospitals for five days. There were reports that some people were badly hurt, unidentified, and unconscious, and therefore unable to alert families of their whereabouts—but there's no good news to find.

Bernie, his wife Barbara, and their four other children instead prepare themselves for a memorial as best they can, but there's a constant crush of people at the Heeran house. Family, friends, and strangers stop by. The word is out—Rockaway has lost a lot of people. Reporters want to talk. At times, it's simply too much, though Billy Heeran and a few friends, some RIBs, are able to find temporary refuge in the ocean. The beach and waters of Rockaway have long offered an escape and sanctuary for those burdened with grief or overwhelmed with troubles.

Just a few days after September 11, the waves are still big. Billy and friends paddle out past the breakers. The waves are big enough to forget the recent nightmare, for just a little while.

No one really forgets. Charlie's friends gather at the house, the Harbor Light, or at the Rugby Clubhouse. They were laughing with him just days ago; now they're remembering him. Charlie was the best rugby wingman they'd ever played with, somebody said. No doubt about it. He'd be the first to buy a round. It was something, the way he lit up a room. He was one of those guys who just made you smile.

To Chris Lawler, Charlie was all those things and more. He was one of his best friends. Chris was in law school, the first steps towards a bright future. He didn't care much about that now. The future was supposed to have Charlie in it. Soon after the memorial mass, Chris posts an on-line tribute on a Web site:

I don't really know how to explain just how special Charlie was, but when God placed him on this earth, we were blessed with an absolute one-of-a-kind person. His abilities were endless and his admirable qualities were immeasurable. You always knew when Charlie entered a room because his charisma immediately filled that room and people took notice.

It was no coincidence that laughs and good times always followed when Charlie burst on the scene. Sean said that Charlie lived to make his friends proud. Well, I will tell you that nothing makes me more proud than to be able to have called Charlie Heeran one of my best friends. I miss you every day, pal.

So does the Harbor Light. It just isn't the same without Charlie. Billy and Sean Heeran work weekends at the bar and do what they can to fill the void, but they know "normal" is a long way off. His father Bernie calls Charlie—named for his grandfather who served under Patton in World War II—a soldier of God and country.

"I didn't want him to go on the fire department. It was too dangerous. But look at what happened," Bernie says, unloading supplies in the parking lot of the Harbor Light. "Charlie was helping other people to the end. I could hear that on the phone. He died a Christian martyr and a patriot—and a firefighter." Whether he knows it or not, Bernie has echoed a quote Charlie selected from an Irish folk song for his high school yearbook: *For I read of our heroes, and wanted the same; to play out my part in the patriot game.*

Normalcy? Not anytime soon. Just ahead are funerals and memorials for John Moran, Henry Miller, Matthew Burke, Eugene Whelan, John Heffernan, and Richie Allen.

▪ Police, rescue workers, and firefighters receive praise for their bravery and heroism, but there's no basking in the adulation. Firefighters, in particular, have burdensome days and nights. They search. They mourn. They visit families. They fight fires. They search for bodies in what they refer to as "The Pile," but what they usually find are grisly remains. A femur. A shoulder. A scalp. A body intact except that the man's feet are missing. Or a head. Sometimes they find an axe or a helmet or some piece of gear. Some firefighters are sent to the roofs of nearby buildings to look for bodies—the bodies of those who jumped from the towers or were aboard the jets that crashed into the buildings.

They mourn for lost friends and their families, but such mourning feels somehow tainted or inadequate. For firefighters, it is a duty and an honor to attend a fellow firefighter's funeral. The mayor, commissioner, and top brass are always there. Thousands of firefighters—in silver-buttoned navy suits, white or navy caps, white gloves, and silver collar pins that proudly give the letters and numbers of the fire companies they represent—line the streets at attention, hands raised in salute. Usually, the full pipe-and-drum band from the FDNY Emerald Society is part of the funeral procession. If a firefighter makes what many call the "ultimate sacrifice," the least the department can do is give the fallen hero a hero's send-off.

Now there are just too many funerals, wakes, and memorial services. On the last Saturday in September, 16 services are held for firefighters in different parts of the city and Long Island. It's impossible to put on the display and show the support that the FDNY is accustomed to delivering. Hundreds of firefighters show, not thousands. The public and firefighters from around the country attend to fill some of the void, but it's not the same. It's a shame, some feel, that there couldn't be a better turnout; the deceased and the family deserved better. It's not supposed to be like this.

There are informal gestures to make as well. Firefighters visit the families of firefighters who were killed. They go just to say hello, to see what they can do. Sometimes they deliver meals they've prepared at the firehouse. Some of these visits are exceptional because they are a matter of duty. The firefighters are told they should notify families that their fathers, husbands, and sons are missing or presumed dead. As a rule, if a firefighter dies in the line of duty, the FDNY chaplain, the commissioner, and company commander will ring the bell to break the news.

Now, the notification process is left up to each individual firehouse. Regular firefighters, sometimes captains or lieutenants, are asked to deliver the news. Of course, most families already know the situation. It won't be a shock to hear the news that their firefighter son, husband, or father is among the missing. Notification is merely a formality, but it is another difficult task heaped on the rank and file.

Tommy Carroll and the men from 219 take the rig to Cathy Brunton's house. They come to show support and wind up needing it themselves. When talk turns to recovery and funerals, Cathy, wife of Captain Vinny Brunton, says, "The captain goes down with his ship. We'll bury Vinny last. He would want to be last, after the other guys are found."

Tommy goes to the kitchen for some water. Jesus, the strength of her! If he stays any longer, he'll start crying. He can't be doing that—not in front of Cathy and her two kids.

The truth is that crying is commonplace for firefighters all over the city. It becomes a familiar yet always gut-wrenching scene. Men in dress uniforms stand stoically on the steps of churches as coffin and pallbearers pass. Then the wife passes, but it's always the kids that get them. The poor kids. All these indomitable men in dress uniforms raise their arms in salute, many with single tears rolling down their faces.

■ And they still have to fight fires. It's September 20, and Tommy's working a regular tour at his firehouse when a call comes in. There's a house fire, a multiple dwelling job on St. John's Place in Brooklyn. Tommy's heart starts pumping immediately. What's waiting for him? Jumpers? A collapse? He knows there's wisdom in getting back on the horse after you've been tossed, but he's thinking that maybe he made all those escapes last week just to die in this fire.

At the scene, Tommy is on the nozzle and enters the burning building—as he's done many times—but now his adrenaline is extreme, as if he's fresh out of Probie school. It's not a big job; it's a regular fire. Everybody around him is working the fire, doing his job. They look steady.

Eventually, the fire is knocked down. For the rest of the shift and the days that follow, Tommy has plenty of time to wonder about whether he's just pressing his luck now. He has to think about transferring to another firehouse, one with fewer reminders of his friends who are no longer here.

■ Chief Hayden has assumed the command of the rescue and recovery task force. It's been a heartbreaking job from the start. There were no survivors found after the first day. Now he sees men he used to work with looking for the bodies of lost sons. He sees sons looking for their fathers, brothers looking for brothers.

■ Matt Tansey remains in tough shape. He's on medical leave with the back and neck injuries. He's lost too many friends to count. He's seen too much for his 27 years. At the wakes for friends Mike Mullan, Angel Juarbe, and Lieutenant Petti, he goes to the caskets and cries until there are no tears left inside.

■ In early October, Tommy has to check the roster journal to make sure he doesn't owe any tours or to see if he has any in the bank. With the crazy scheduling that's been going on for the last month, he's lost track. By chance, he flips open the thick, black book to September 11, 2001. He's struck by the names. There he is, "Carroll." Then the other names: Miller, Brunton, O'Berg, Kelly, Chipura, Palumbo, and Linnane.

Again, he starts thinking that it's time to go to a different firehouse, finish off the couple of years before retirement—somewhere easy, a place where emotions don't so often and suddenly knock you off your feet—but he can't do that. Not with this list of names staring back at him. He's not going anywhere. Not for a while, if ever. It'd be a bad example to the younger guys who've just come to this firehouse. You just can't get up and leave when things are tough.

■ Gallows humor, often a reflex in Rockaway, is muted. Maybe the locals are waiting for the firefighters' lead on this. Firefighters often engage in dark humor to deal with everyday horrors, but they're reserved; right now, they just don't feel like laughing. When *they* laugh, the people will laugh, too.

Mike Moran, whose brother John was killed, breaks the ice.

On stage, at the Paul McCartney-sponsored "Concert for New York" at Madison Square Garden on October 20, Moran is invited onstage to introduce a band. As the music begins, Moran steps up to the microphone and says to the sold-out arena and huge TV audience, "And I want to say one more thing in the spirit of the Irish people. Osama Bin Laden, you can kiss my royal Irish ass. And I live in Rockaway! And this is my face, bitch!"

The dare is met by wild applause and chants of *"USA! USA!"* Millions more learn of Moran the next day on front pages and radio shows across the country.

With the levity introduced by Moran, Rockaway's George Johnson is fair play. In the fine FDNY tradition, he goes from hero to punch line. George, one of the three firefighters in the famous flag-raising photo, is the one on the left, hands on hips, watching Old Glory being raised amidst the rubble. His brethren take the celebrated and revered photo, and doctor it up so George is looking skyward at the flag—but now he's wearing nothing but a Speedo.

The picture is faxed to the many firehouses where George is known. Although he resists virtually all media requests for interviews, and would just as soon become an anonymous firefighter once again, George enjoys a gag photo in *The Wave.* About 15 Rockaway rugby pals honor him by snapping a photo of themselves, all with hands on hips, looking skyward at a flag.

Mark Cannon, who spends a good chunk of the summer in Rockaway playing basketball with the Graybeards, tells the story of being on the Staten Island ferry, crammed with people wearing life jackets, looking up at the two towers on fire. As the ferry is about to leave the dock, the south tower falls. People on the boat bawl and screech in wild hysterics. The ferry gets blanketed with black smoke and dust.

A few minutes elapse, the cloud lifts, the crowd—mostly quiet now—is stunned as the ferry starts towards Staten Island. A young woman identifies herself to Cannon as a reporter; she asks him if he'd mind answering a question. He shrugs.

She takes out a pad and pen, and asks, "Have you ever seen anything like this before?" It's such an absurd question that it makes Cannon pause. He wonders if she's kidding. She's not. Maybe she's in shock.

Later, Cannon thinks to himself, Well, if she had only asked that question a half hour later, I would've been able to say, As a matter of fact, I have.

Humor and light-hearted anecdotes are rare. No one feels like laughing all that much.

■ Firefighters do their best to get to as many funerals and memorials as they can. It seems that over the weeks, the services grow longer—as if mourners have more time to compose themselves and more time to write longer eulogies. One service lasts four hours. There are 11 eulogizers. You can say that at least you're not in the coffin, or that's not your loved one, and that's true, but it's draining nonetheless.

At the same time, strength comes from unexpected sources. Shrines are built at the doors and sidewalks of many firehouses. Neighbors and strangers, people just passing by, place candles, photos, and flowers on the sidewalk outside. Lunches and dinners arrive from private citizens and from restaurants.

A beer truck pulls up to every firehouse in Brooklyn and Queens. "Take as many cases as you can," the driver says. "It's on the boss."

They can't eat all the homemade cookies that come from neighbors. Schoolchildren from across the country send drawings and cards to firehouses. One second-grader draws a picture of firefighters and writes, "It's up to you to save America."

Many people come by with money. Sometimes donations come from a group, perhaps a block association or some kind of club. Sometimes individuals stop and hand over cash or checks. Give it to the families who need it, okay? Most firehouses have to open up accounts to keep track of all the donations. Some firefighters tell people the money would be better given to others. The FDNY widows and children will be okay, they say. If you can find the families of security guards, bus boys, receptionists, or clerks— they'll need all the help they can get.

At Tommy Carroll's 219, 105 firehouse where seven men perished, donations are steady and sometimes overwhelming. Tommy is never more touched than when three or four kids, probably from the projects, stand at the firehouse door waiting for a firefighter to appear so they can donate their baseball and basketball trophies . . . their prized possessions. Here they are, these dirt-poor kids, offering their trophies. It's a simple, beautiful gesture. The trophies are placed prominently on a shelf on the first floor of the firehouse.

Three big, black women, each in their Sunday best, walk along a street in Brooklyn. A firefighter cracks, "They're on their way to the Church of Nell Carter."

To his surprise, they march into the firehouse and take turns giving bear hugs to the wisecracking firefighter. "Honey, you better get used to this, 'cause we ain't never gonna stop."

Firefighters usually rescue and help strangers—people they don't know, people they'll never see or hear from again. Now, in a world that couldn't look bleaker, strangers are helping firefighters.

With the gifts and gestures come tributes. Firefighters are heroes. In a sense, each one is like the Hollywood actor struggling for years and then suddenly becomes an "overnight" success. Firefighters are suddenly discovered. They're our true heroes. It's a tag many find uplifting yet uncomfortable; well intentioned yet disconcerting.

Flip Mullen, retired for years and out with a back injury, donned his old firefighting gear and raced into the city on September 11. He deflects praise and tells a writer, "You should do a story about the ironworkers. Those guys are unbelievable. They're busting their asses trying to find people or bodies so families can have some peace in their lives. They climb up these beams. One wrong step and they're dead. And they cut and burn their way through all this shit."

Another firefighter waves off the adulation, too. "Before September 11, we were schmucks in bumblebee coats. Now we're heroes? Come on. You want to call the 343 who died heroes? Okay, but not the rest of us."

Heroism, it seems, is in the eye of the beholder. Perhaps it's a sign of the times, but after a catastrophe or epic event, there is a societal reflex to keep score. Who did what? Who gets credit? Medals have to be awarded and then who gets the blame? Fingers have to be pointed.

At first blush, an argument about what a hero is can seem foolish or petty, but it's complex and the cause of some consternation among firefighters. One firefighter, who works at a house that lost several men, said, "Hey, most times it's great to be called a hero, but why are people calling us that now? Because our friends died. I feel guilty being called a hero. People offered us free vacations, tickets to games, all this stuff and that's great, but how am I supposed to enjoy any of that? It's being offered because 343 brothers died."

Another firefighter accepts what comes. "Three words, 'zeroes for heroes,'" he says, referring to what cops and firefighters see as an infamous contract negotiated by Mayor Giuliani and the unions in his first term. It was called "zeroes for heroes" by the rank and file because it offered 0% raises from 1995 through 1997. "The city was flush and we got squat. I don't like the timing, but if something's offered, we should take it. We should take it for all the years we did stuff and got squat."

Over beers at a table at the Harbor Light, the conversation about heroes reflects how divergent and nuanced the topic can be. "Some people act bravely because they really want a medal or to get their picture in the paper. It's no more complicated than that."

"That's right," another firefighter says. "Sometimes it's not about self-sacrifice, it's about personal gain. Some things that look brave are really selfish acts."

"Though if it's your ass being saved, you ain't gonna complain," another guys says, causing knowing laughs in the group.

And so it goes. Some believe the heroes are the rescuers who died; some say we'll never know the heroes. What about the office worker who stopped to help a co-worker? Maybe they died. We'll never know. They won't get a hero's funeral. You start calling some heroes, you're going to neglect others who deserve praise, too.

A civilian still insists on paying tribute to his firefighter friends. "What they say is true. When others are running out of burning buildings, you guys run in."

"That's our job."

"Bullshit! It's more than that. Sixty. *Sixty,*" he repeats, "firefighters who died were off duty. Talk about heroes."

It's enough for everyone to pause and take a sip of beer. "Well, I still want to say that you're not just a hero because you put on a uniform."

That sounds right, but someone argues that it's not so simple. "You make a heroic gesture the day you take the oath. You pledge to serve and protect the community. Putting on the uniform makes you part of a team. Without a team in place, there'd be a lot less heroes." That sounds right, too, but there's nuance here as well.

"The pledge is bullshit. The uniform can be misleading. You think you're part of a team, but you're alone more times than you want to admit. Yeah, everybody took the oath. You think everybody took it seriously? I've seen a lot of guys who coast, sit back, avoid any kind of danger. They're absolute loads. They got it down to a science. The uniform? Gimme a break. You got guys in uniforms who got where they are by taking tests. They never get their hands dirty. They send others into danger and they're wearing uniforms, too. But are *they* heroes?"

"Who knows," another guys says. "To me, heroes are the people who give you a cold drink, wipe your face, show kindness. We may be running in to save strangers, but I go in thinking those strangers are heroes. Know what I mean? I'm thinking I might be going in to help somebody who, turns out, will make a difference in this world. Even if it's just a guy who does right by his kids, puts food on the table. That's what I think in my sane moments."

A firefighter at the end of the table says his heroes are guys on the fire department who fight to make firefighting safer. The guys who push for better equipment and tighter building codes; the guys who pass down wisdom and experience. "It's safer now 'cause of those guys. They've saved lives and nobody thinks about it." Everyone at the table, a mix of firefighters and civilians, takes a moment to think about the point.

"Tell ya the truth, I'm glad we don't talk about this hero bullshit too much. It usually means another funeral."

"Yeah, but you know," another civilian says, "firefighters aren't heroes because they died. You guys are heroes because of what you do every day." There's a collective groan. They can't take the compliments.

A firefighter shrugs. "Hey, there's worse things than being called a hero. My brother-in-law's got a monster wallet. He makes a truckload of dough. All these years, I've been hearing about how great he is, just 'cause he makes money." His eyes twinkle. "Now everybody thinks I'm the man."

A firefighter almost spits out his beer. "The *man*? Yeah, yeah. Don't forget when you and your brother-in-law meet St. Peter at the pearly gates. He'll ask him, 'What'd you do?' He'll say, 'I made money.' Then he'll ask you, and you'll say 'I helped save people.'"

Another firefighter puts up a hand. "I know, I know. St. Peter will say, 'Stop showing off, stop bragging. Stand over here and wait. You were just doing your job.'"

A civilian raises his bottle. "All right, all right, you're *not* heroes, but I ain't calling Michael Jordan or Derek Jeter next time my house is on fire!"

■ Halloween in Rockaway is usually full-spirited fun. Many homes are dressed in store-bought cobwebs. Homemade ghouls on front lawns and porches spook passers-by. Hundreds of kids go door to door for treats. Teenagers are in charge of tricks. By the end of the day, it looks like there's been a blizzard of silly string and shaving cream. At night, people go to Fort Tilden for a hayride through the dark back roads of the fort. Witches and goblins jump from behind trees and bushes to give everyone a good scare.

Not this year. This year, the frights are real. Government alerts are issued about the possibility that a new round of terrorism might occur. Anthrax is sent through the mail to several media companies and elected officials. There's just too much real world this year to have any kind of fun on Halloween.

■ It had been a different summer for Richie Allen. Usually, come June, he'd be climbing a lifeguard chair on Rockaway Beach. This past June, he was climbing ladders as a new graduate of the Fire Academy.

After first passing a written and then a physical exam, newly appointed members of the FDNY report to the Fire Academy or "Probie School" on Randall's Island—a 27-acre island between Manhattan, the Bronx, and Queens in the East River. For many, it will be their first exposure to the firefighting life. The recruits face 13 weeks of physical drills and classroom instruction with military or boot camp overtones. Much of the instruction comes from active firefighters—men and women who have taken a detail from their regular firehouses to offer knowledge and experience to the recruits.

A typical day might mean a morning run, followed by calisthenics and work-related drills. Probies will line up in bunker gear and receive orders about the day's assignment, which will vary from day to day. There's a lot to learn, and there's usually one right way and a lot of wrong ways. Probies must know how to properly ascend a 100-foot aerial ladder, operate and stretch hose lines, conduct rope rescues, familiarize themselves with and know how to use tools. They're also expected to learn firefighting tactics and emergency medical procedures. They won't graduate unless they pass weekly tests, a mid-term, and a final exam.

When they do graduate, probationary firefighters are ready to join the ranks of New York's Bravest. However, they are, after all, still Probies, and they'll be Probies until their first-year anniversary of joining the fire department. Although official rules and guidelines change from time to time, the life of a new graduate is uncertain. Probies might spend seven weeks in a ladder company, then seven weeks at an engine, and then head back to Randall's Island—also known as The Rock—for supplementary training.

No matter where they spend their time, Probies are expected to do grunt work and chores—sweeping floors, making beds, doing errands. It's as much a tradition as a rite of passage in firehouses. Smart Probies will accept the tasks, generally keep quiet, and listen to the senior guys. Although probationary firefighters are deemed ready when they arrive at a firehouse, they'll benefit beyond words from the tutelage of senior guys.

The senior guys are the ones who'll make the difference when it comes to learning how to fight a "real fire." Any firefighter will tell you that all the training in the world will only prepare you so much for the real thing. At the Fire Academy, they'll test you in "smoke rooms" and place you in stressful situations, but a corner of the brain knows safety measures are in place. They've done this before. They don't want anyone to be killed or hurt.

A real fire, in a house or store or factory, won't be controlled or supervised. They'll be no way of knowing if there's structural damage, or if a floor or ceiling will collapse without warning. There'll be no way to know if hazardous materials might be stowed illegally, and it's impossible to say what role adrenaline will play. The unknowns make it a crapshoot.

That's why some of the best learning will come on the job, from the senior guys who say, "Come here, kid. This is how you do it." That's when the senior guy gets down on his knees and crawls in, and the Probie follows into a dark, hot place. They'll stay low and maybe spot a source of fire, or find a room no one knew was there. Maybe they'll find someone who needs help. It could last just a few minutes, but it'll top anything they learned at the academy.

Probies know they have to be tested. They can't wait for their first real fire. Richie Allen felt that way. Richie, 31 years old—a Probie at Manhattan's Engine 4, Ladder 15—had finished the academy two months before and couldn't wait for his first big job.

It finally came on September 11. His first fire gave him his lasting legacy: he gave his life to save others.

A memorial was held at St. Francis for Richie on November 9. The Allen family, like many Catholic families, prefers funerals, but funerals are held when a body is present; when there is no body, memorials are conducted in memory of the person.

Richie's uncle, Bobby McGuire—a firefighter as well—had searched the ruins for two months to find the body to no avail. Rescue workers became familiar with Richie's name. A firefighter from Rockaway Beach, Chris Bach, had etched a simple message in the dust at numerous places around Ground Zero. "Pray for Richie Allen. He died for you!"

Richie, a lifelong Rockaway guy, was a New York City teacher and a beach lifeguard before becoming a firefighter. Richie was also part of a well-known family in the area. He was grandson to John McGuire, brother of Basketball Hall of Fame members Dick and Al McGuire. The family was known for owning the 101 Deli, where you'd get the best hero sandwich on the way to the beach.

The church and street outside were packed with mourners that Friday morning. Coincidentally, the Concorde supersonic jet resumed commercial flights to and from JFK airport the same day as Allen's memorial service. It had been grounded for the previous 15 months after a fatal crash in Paris. The 15 months were a welcome respite for Rockawayites who had endured the deafening noise of the jets for more than a quarter century. Although air traffic above Rockaway is steady, many of the planes fly high enough to be out of earshot. The Concorde flies low and loud. *Very* loud. The harsh roar can shake house foundations and set off car alarms.

Allen's would be the 11th memorial or funeral service at St. Francis de Sales Church for victims of the World Trade Center attacks of September 11; others had been held at nearby parishes and funeral homes. Allen's was the last on the church's schedule.

Some families were holding off on funerals or memorials, waiting for bodies to be recovered or to receive notification that positive identification was made through DNA (deoxyribonucleic acid) testing. In any event, it looked liked there would be a break of sorts, nothing scheduled until after Thanksgiving and Christmas.

It proved to be a short weekend.

CHAPTER 6

Not Again—
Flight 587 Crashes

March 1968

The numbers are hard to believe. More than 39 million people visited Rockaway in the summer of 1951. That's more than the number of people who visit the State of Florida each year. The Rockaway peninsula, half as long as Manhattan, drew millions through the 1950s, as crowds sought amusement arcades and sandy beaches. Hotels, from the glorious to the fleabag, accommodated the vacationers.

The parking lot at Riis Park Beach can hold 10,000 cars. By noon on weekends, the lot was usually filled. Photographs from the era show happy sunbathers and an inviting ocean, but sand is rarely seen—it's covered by the massive crowd.

Gradually, it wasn't so hard to find a place for your blanket on the beach. The automobile, now owned by more and more families, allowed travel to Long Island and New Jersey beaches. Some people started installing air conditioning units in their homes; some made investments in backyard pools. For years, crowds had gone to the beach for the cool relief offered by ocean waves and fresh breezes. With alternatives just as cool and inviting, fewer people headed to Rockaway. As crowds started to dwindle, some businesses folded and hotels couldn't fill their rooms. It wasn't long before parts of Rockaway had that worn, run-down, used-to-be-somebody look.

Fires destroyed Colonial Hall, the Majestic, and the Arverne Hotel, and one splendid and not-so-splendid hotel after another. Some were called "suspicious"; others had always been firetraps waiting for a reason to ignite. Unlike after the great fires of Rockaway past, none of them was replaced. Rooms were going empty as it was—there was no reason to rebuild.

If there was any hope for a revival, the City of New York snuffed it out. Although it seemed contrary to common sense, the city apparently didn't view the beach as an asset, but more as a depot for its urban ills. Rather than protect and promote one of the few New York communities that could boast a wide-open—even stunning—oceanfront, the city dotted the area with housing projects.

In 1951, 410 units called the Arverne Houses were built; four years later, the Hammel Houses with 712 units opened. In 1959, the Redfern Houses with 604 units opened at the eastern end of the peninsula, just at the border of Queens and Nassau Counties. Redfern looked like a fortress between the two counties, but it wasn't clear if the fortress walls were to keep people in or out of Rockaway. Finally, in 1961, the hulking Edgemere Houses and its 1,395 units went up and loomed over the mid-section of the peninsula with all the charm of a penitentiary, which is what it looked like.

The coup de grace was the Arverne Renewal Project. In the early 1960s, the city decided to start from scratch. Someone in city government apparently thought the oceanfront property might be worth an investment. The city moved to declare some 300 acres "condemned" and went to work razing homes, hotels, and cottages.

It was a decision that seems absurd today. The "condemned" property included handsome homes with open porches and plentiful windows. Cupolas, turrets, and large bay windows were found on homes throughout Arverne. Though some buildings in the area were decaying—giving the city the excuse it needed to call it a slum—the entire area would probably be landmarked today, so impressive were the homes and cottages. Not impressive, of course, to autocrat Robert Moses, the aggressive urban planner. Arverne just happened to be the last of a series of sites Moses had targeted for clearance, and no one could stop him.

Heartbroken owners watched as the bulldozers moved in on homes with wraparound porches. Casting shadows over the demolition were the housing projects that remained intact and untouched.

Then the city ran out of money.

Forty years later, the area is a fallow, desolate wasteland. The renewal remains stillborn. Fresh, ocean air blows through overgrown weeds and garbage. Worn car tires are everywhere; washing machine parts stick out of the sand. Packs of wild dogs make their home among stained mattresses and burned out automobile chassis. Though there's new talk of development—there always is—the area remains the largest tract of city-owned vacant land in New York.

A few miles west, the Riis Park parking lot is free of the garbage and wild dogs, but the place that used to overflow with cars is just as desolate as the Arverne Renewal Area. Rockaway, the place that once drew 2.5 million people on a single weekend, was lucky to get 100,000 by the late 1990s.

The automobile hurt Rockaway's tourism trade, no doubt, but, unlike other tourist destinations, Rockaway could not adapt—not while the city was establishing the peninsula as a dumping ground. The city effectively killed Rockaway as an attraction and, perhaps worse, separated the peninsula along racial and cultural lines.

The city's urban planners had split the peninsula into city on the east end and suburb on the west. By leveling the 300 acres in Arverne and not rebuilding, the city left the eastern half of the peninsula saturated with public housing and vacant lots. The other half, the western end— which included Rockaway Beach, Rockaway Park, Belle Harbor, and Breezy Point—tilted towards the other extreme as fine, year-round, one- and two-family houses were built.

The city's actions also triggered the hasty decline of Far Rockaway High School, once a top school. No less than three eventual Nobel Prize winners came from its graduating ranks: Richard Feynman (the renowned physicist who developed much of the mathematics behind the atomic bomb) was a Far Rockaway graduate, as was Baruch Blumberg (prize winner for mathematics) and Burton Richter (physics). Dr. Joyce Brothers, corporate financier Carl Ichan, publisher Fred Drasner, and

*several professional athletes were among those who attended the school in
its halcyon days.*

*If there were any lingering doubts that Rockaway was finished as a
resort area, the final curtain fell on March 31, 1968. The last remnant of
its glory days went up in smoke as Curley's Atlas Hotel on the boardwalk at Beach 116th Street was wiped out by a monstrous fire.*

*Curley's was an institution of sorts, low to middle brow, a sprawling
place that might be called kitschy today. Comedian George Carlin, recalling his hardscrabble youth, wryly notes on his official Web site that he
was conceived in Curley's in August 1936. No description would be
complete without saying it was popular. Vacationers rented rooms during the summer season, while DFDs rented umbrellas and beach chairs
from the concessions Curley's operated on the ground floor and at various stations along the beach.*

*Curley's faced the ocean and ran the length of the block between Beach
116th and 117th Streets. For many local kids, Curley's meant their first
job. They'd get something called "working papers"—Department of
Labor permits allowing kids 14 and older to get jobs. Most kids hoped to
land the jobs behind the counter, selling hot dogs and soda, or at the
beach umbrella concession stand. No such luck. Rookies were invariably
given a large box with shoulder straps, and sent to hawk ice cream and
orange drinks on the sand. Dry ice kept the items cool but made trudging
through the sand that much tougher for the young vendors.*

*In early spring of 1968, before the hotel opened for the season, three
seven-year-old boys played with matches and set small fires under the
wooden ramp that led from the boardwalk into Curley's. Like so many old
structures, Curley's was made of wood and was easily ignitable. Within
minutes, fire ran up the face of the building like a flag up a pole, then
spread out like a book across the entire front.*

*Neighborhood residents—Pete Brady, Steve Stathis, and his brother
Whipper—converged on the beach to watch the spectacular blaze and
were pushed back to the ocean's edge by the radiant heat. A handful of
surfers, catching early spring waves, stayed in the water, sitting on their
boards, struck by the climbing wall of fire just off the boardwalk. A
young cop, Flip Mullen, who'd become a firefighter in a couple of years,
kept the street crowd from getting too close to the fire.*

Four hundred and fifty firefighters with 61 pieces of equipment battled to control the fire, but, as with other Rockaway conflagrations, strong winds conspired with the fire. Embers flew across Beach 116th Street causing the roof of the Rockaway Beach Hotel to ignite. The two bridges to Rockaway—the Marine Park Bridge and the Crossbay—were closed to all but emergency vehicles. Curley's may as well have been made from ice cream sticks. The fire ate up the rickety wood structure for more than five hours, leaving Curley's in ashes and the Rockaway Beach Hotel badly damaged.

Curley's was gone and so was an era. Thirty years later, a vacant sand-and-gravel lot sits, unused, on the oceanfront. The handful of smaller hotels that remained were converted into single-room occupancy or welfare hotels.

November 2001

American flags have always flown in Rockaway. In Belle Harbor, the words "For God, For Country" are inscribed on the tan brick wall above a doorway on the St. Francis de Sales School building. Voters tend to send democrats to office. U.S. Senator Chuck Schumer cut his teeth as a congressman, thanks to Rockaway voters who sent him to Washington for nine straight terms. Voters never quite held it against him that he never delivered on his promise of a swimming pool for Riis Park or better public schools. Rockaway voters aren't surprised to know that Schumer has a reputation among colleagues for being a publicity hound. He was always in *The Wave*. His successor, Anthony Weiner, hasn't had a meaningful challenge from a republican, and it's unlikely he ever will. Barring any surprising development, Weiner—who voters find energetic, quick on his feet, and able—will be able to hold the seat for as long as wishes.

Rockaway voters are not blindly democratic, though. There are plenty of Ronald Reagan democrats and hordes of those who voted for Rudolph Giuliani in his three mayoral tries. Voters supported republican Michael Bloomberg, New York's current mayor, while also pulling the lever for the democrat in the city council race.

Through the years, many of those voters have flown the red, white, and blue on pleasant days and holidays. However, in the aftermath of September 11, there are flags flying on almost every house. Local shops quickly ran out of what admittedly began with a modest supply of flags. Some homeowners are embarrassed because they don't have a ready flag, so they tape cutout newspaper flags to their front windows or hang posters with pro-American slogans on front doors. Automobiles fly flags from their antennas; some of those cars have FDNY bumper stickers: "Some Gave All; All Gave Some."

There are other pictures and tributes: a firefighter and a cop in their uniforms stand tall among the buildings of lower Manhattan. They are the new Twin Towers. A neighborhood pub adorns its front window with a *New York Post* front page blaring a "Dead or Alive" headline over the shadowy countenance of Osama Bin Laden. There's another bumper sticker with an American flag and the words: "These Colors Don't Run."

In the lobby at the bank, on a bulletin board at the gym, on telephone poles, and on fireplace mantles and front doors, you'll be sure to see the photo of the three firefighters raising the American flag in the rubble of Ground Zero. The three men remained firm in their shared belief that it was merely a morale booster, a gesture to their fallen brothers. They sought neither fame nor glory, nor financial gain.

The flag-raising was spontaneous, and a photographer just happened to catch the moment that was reminiscent of the Iwo Jima image. Coincidentally, both flags came from a boat. The Iwo Jima flag came from a ship, one that was sunk during the Pearl Harbor attack; the one at Ground Zero came from a yacht docked in a marina behind the World Financial Center. Although the three firefighters have been to the White House, had a postage stamp issued in their honor, and were sent to the USS *Theodore Roosevelt* on behalf of the FDNY to retrieve the flag, which had been on loan, it's a measure of their modesty that their names are not well known. One of the three said he didn't know the names of the men who raised the flag at Iwo Jima, and he hoped most people would never learn his.

In Rockaway, people are pleased that one of the three firefighters is a local, but they don't make a fuss over it. They seem to accept the picture much the way George and the other two—Dan McWilliams and William Eisengrein—would like it to be accepted. It's proud and heartfelt. They're glad it's "a shot in the arm" that the country seems to need, but it doesn't make them more heroic than others.

Of course, Rockaway was already proud of George. In 1996, a four-year-old boy from a small town in Kentucky was suffering from life-threatening leukemia. After nearly three years of unsuccessful chemotherapy, he was in desperate need of a bone marrow transplant. When no one in his family matched his marrow type, his parents enrolled young Forrest Nichols in the National Marrow Donor Program's registry.

Rockaway, like many towns, held a donor drive—free coffee and donuts for some of your blood. Firefighter George Johnson, then a six-year veteran of the FDNY, was identified as a match. Finding a match through blood work is good news, but the healthy person has to agree to the procedure. Serious complications are rare but could include adverse anesthesia, transfusion reactions, or infection. Donating requires a short hospital stay, and the subsequent pain in the lower back and fatigue can last for several days or longer. It's one thing to do it for a family member or friend; donating marrow for a stranger is something else. Yet, without hesitation, George made his healthy bone marrow available, and a few months later helped save the life of Forrest Nichols.

Unsurprisingly to those who know him, George downplayed his contribution. George might tell you he's a wonder to behold on the rugby field, but he won't say much about his selfless, inspiring, truly laudable actions—like being part of the famous photo. Although George, McWilliams, and Eisengrein say very little, their image is lasting and uplifting.

Even people who are usually comfortable as committed cynics make gestures of solidarity and patriotism. They go to prayer vigils and fundraisers; they wear red, white, and blue pins on their lapels; they download Kate Smith's "God Bless America" from a Web site. The local branch of the Knights of Columbus raises $65,000 from neighbors who attend a benefit and open their wallets for the families of victims. Aid comes from the Rockaway Artists Alliance, the chamber of commerce, bars, restaurants, bake sales, and block associations.

Steve Stathis calls all his basketball friends, the Graybeards, together. It's occurred to him that, because so many of the players are coaches, referees, firefighters, and ready volunteers for community service, there might be wisdom in making the group something more formalized than a bunch of guys who get together for basketball and occasional beers or barbecues.

Fifty men quickly sign on to the idea. They establish themselves as not-for-profit and begin raising money for families in need. They meet regularly to brainstorm because they want to do more than raise funds. Their efforts and goals mirror other groups in Rockaway, and many around the country for that matter. There's an unprecedented spike in volunteerism and other forms of altruism.

Monsignor Geraghty, although a superb public speaker, resists much of the media, which are eager to pluck from him any anecdote, any insight. Some press him about body counts. One reporter approaches him and begins by saying he's heard that 130 children in the school have lost parents. Geraghty says that's not true.

The reporter asks, "How many?"

Geraghty says, "I'm not sure of the number, but I know that number is not true."

The reporter presses him. "How do you know it's not true? Can you give us the names and phone numbers of families who've lost someone?"

Even though Geraghty avoids as many microphones, notepads, and pens as he can, the story of this devastated parish on a peninsula on the outskirts of New York City works its way through the country. More than $135,000 in cash and checks arrives in the mail at St. Francis from places such as rural South Carolina and Iowa; from California and Massachusetts; from Texas and Rhode Island.

Geraghty is proud of the brick-framed memorial on the lawn outside the church. Installed decades ago, it depicts the "Immortal Chaplains"—four men of different faiths who gave their lives in World War II and who were posthumously awarded a special Congressional Medal of Valor in 1960.

Clark Poling, the youngest, was a congregationalist minister. George Fox, the oldest, was a Methodist minister, a decorated veteran of World War I. Johnny Washington was a Roman Catholic priest who, before the war, had worked with boys in an inner-city parish. Alexander Goode was a Jewish rabbi who had also been going to medical school.

Soon after the United States entered World War II, independent of each other, they became army chaplains. In January 1943, they sailed with 900 troops on the USS *Dorchester*, bound for Europe. On a frigid February morning, just 150 miles from their destination, the ship was torpedoed. The hit was decisive and deadly. The ship began taking water and started to sink.

Aboard the *Dorchester*, panic and chaos set in. Men jumped from the ship into lifeboats, overcrowding them and capsizing some. The four chaplains attempted to calm and comfort those still on board. They opened a storage locker and began distributing life jackets. When there were no more life jackets in the storage room, the chaplains removed theirs and gave them to four frightened young men.

Geraghty knows that, when giving their life jackets, Rabbi Goode did not call out for a Jew, Father Washington did not call out for a Catholic, nor did the Reverends Fox and Poling call out for a Protestant. They simply gave their life jackets to the next man in line. Like firefighters and rescuers of all kinds, they didn't first consider creed or color.

As the ship went down, survivors in nearby rafts could see the four chaplains, arms linked, praying.

The memorial on the lawn is cross-denominational and so is the generosity of strangers. Donations come from Jews, Catholics, Protestants, atheists, and the unsure. Some envelopes have $5; some have $500. Stirring, heart-wrenching letters accompany many of the donations. Some donations are pieces of artwork, such as lithographs. A framed, handmade "knot board" arrives from New Mexico. Fastened in the frame are roped knots such as the "Grapewine" or the "Flemish bend," each one accompanied by a spiritual adage or poem.

Geraghty is stunned by the generosity of strangers and enlightened about the positive side of media coverage. Many of the notes with the donations comment about how important it is for them to give as directly as they can to the victims rather than to a massive charity. They tell him they know he'll get the money to people who need it and they're right. He's only too happy to present the donations to families of children in the school who've lost a parent in the September 11 attacks.

Geraghty finds himself more than a conduit; he's a beneficiary as well. He makes new friends across the country, such as Father Jamail of St. Vincent de Paul parish in Houston, Texas. Jamail is dying of cancer, Geraghty learns, but he's got enough strength to inspire Geraghty. Geraghty finds himself further rewarded by the message brought by a Catholic layman from Jamail's parish. A man named John Connolly contacted Geraghty after reading about St. Francis in the newspapers, and told the Monsignor that they've taken up a collection in his parish church of St. Vincent de Paul for the affected families of St. Francis. Connolly adds that he and his family will be in New York, and would like to visit Geraghty and perhaps meet some of the people in Belle Harbor. He'll bring the check with him.

Geraghty suggests that Connolly and his family come to Sunday mass, and that he'd introduce him to the congregants at noon mass. "Tell ya what," Geraghty says, "even better, why don't you present me with the check at mass."

On that Sunday, Geraghty meets Connolly before mass and asks if he'd like to address the church audience as well. Connolly, wearing a light windbreaker, tells him that he's a little nervous about speaking before a large crowd. However, when Geraghty calls him to come from the pew to present the check, if he has his jacket off, he'll speak.

In the middle of mass, Geraghty stands at the pulpit telling the Sunday worshippers about this generous parish in Houston, Texas. Geraghty knows how to work a crowd. He informs them that a family—the Connollys—representing St. Vincent de Paul, is here to present the donation, and that John Connolly will come to the altar with a check to benefit the parish children who lost parents on September 11.

As soon as he calls Connolly to the altar, applause echoes throughout the church. Geraghty puts up a hand for silence. "Oh, John, while you're standing there, I should tell everyone that the check is for $40,000." There's a collective gasp and then a booming ovation.

Connolly, it so happens, has his jacket off, so Geraghty motions towards the lectern. The church quiets as the man from Texas looks out at unfamiliar faces.

"I'm here. My wife and children are here from St. Vincent de Paul parish to let you know you're not alone. We're here because we love you. This is what it means to be Catholic. This is who we are. We just want you to know, you're not alone."

■ There's a different feeling this Veteran's Day in Belle Harbor. The country is at war. The United States has been attacked. Most of the firefighters and cops who live in Rockaway aren't veterans of the armed services but, this year—just two months after the World Trade Center attack—it certainly seems as if they're deserving of recognition. They were the first on the scene in a time of war. They raced to save others, and they kept coming to the unstable site to rescue those who might be trapped or hurt. They responded, not knowing if the attacks were over.

Firefighters, cops, and emergency responders of all kinds were ground troops on September 11. It sure seems as if they're veterans.

In Rockaway, it'll be a day without bagpipes. Richie Allen's memorial the Friday before would be the last one for a while. After daily mass at 9 AM, St. Francis will be quiet. No funerals, memorials, or school for that matter. The kids are home on this Monday because it's Veteran's Day. It's a clear, beautiful day with a steady ocean breeze. There's a slight chill in the air, just enough to let you know the seasons will, in fact, change. For some, it's a good day to sleep late or run errands.

■ Kenny Whelan, captain of Ladder 137 on Beach 116th Street, has the day off. Not to worry. Billy Gallagher is the lieutenant in charge. If he's going to worry, it'll be about his mother, Eileen, who's in the car with him and his wife, Roseanne. They're on Manhattan's FDR Drive, taking mom to Lenox Hill Hospital for a vascular procedure to relieve blockage in her carotid arteries. They say it's not that big a deal, but it is her neck. How can that *not* be a big deal?

■ Tommy Carroll is home, a day off; Eileen's at work. T.J. has just started playing golf, so he's up and out already, eager to go with a buddy and his dad to a course about 20 minutes away. Brianne's had a sleep-over, which means she and her friend, Patrice, stayed up too late talking. They're still asleep. Tommy takes a glance at the kitchen clock. Maybe he can run Sean over to the outdoor roller rink for some skating practice.

■ Peter Brady and Billy Collins are in Staten Island today. They've been sent to "terrorist response training" drills set up by the FDNY.

■ George Johnson and five other firefighters from Ladder 157 in Brooklyn are volunteering their time to fill in for Ladder 15 at the South Street Seaport in lower Manhattan. It's another example of firefighters "stepping up"—a firefighter's phrase for doing the right thing. The city will give fire companies the day off for a funeral but not for a wake. To allow the Ladder 15 firefighters the chance to go to a wake scheduled that day, George and the others are there to cover their shifts.

■ Chief Hayden is just Pete or Petey to old friends today—no deputy chief. He's out walking his dog, enjoying his first day off in two months. He has spent every day at Ground Zero since September 11.

■ Tom McVeigh slaps $200 on the table. Lunch and dinner is his treat today, his last one on the job. He's finishing his life in The Big House—the Far Rockaway firehouse that gets its name because it holds two engines and a truck, and it's a third bigger than any double house. It's a big building, too; with the extra engine, it houses more people as well. Single houses might just have five guys working a shift; The Big House has 15. McVeigh was supposed to be finished by late September or early October, but he put things on temporary hold after September 11. He arrived for work at 6 PM the night before, and he'll be walking out a retired firefighter by 6 PM tonight. A good way to remember Veteran's Day.

■ Billy Heeran is at work, sitting before a bank of computer and TV screens. The market is about to open. His brother, Sean, is at work a few blocks over. He has his eye on the NASDAQ.

■ Matt Tansey is sleeping at his parent's house, his girlfriend next to him. The last two months have been hell, but he's starting to feel better and a little more hopeful. He's been swimming, doing some yoga, doing what he can—short of surgery—for that herniated disk in his neck.

■ Steve Stathis has the day off from Con Ed, and he uses the free time to shoot over a few blocks to Beach 116th Street to straighten out an insurance matter with his broker and friend, Dickie Roberts. He's done and back in his car by 9:10 AM.

■ Bernie Heeran, father of Billy and Sean, is home. He has week-end receipts from the Harbor Light and a stack of bills spread over his bed. A loud roar starts building. Must be the damn Concorde.

■ Kevin Lunny is sliding a foot into a pair of dress pants. He has to be in Massapequa, Long Island for a memorial service for Anthony Jovic, an FDNY lieutenant killed on September 11.

■ Whipper Stathis is at his firehouse in Howard Beach, a 12-minute drive from Rockaway.

■ Monsignor Geraghty is saying 9 o'clock mass at St. Francis de Sales Church.

■ Alex, Mike, and Mark are early for CYO basketball practice scheduled for 9:30 AM. The three seventh graders stand outside the school gym, hoping the coach will show up early and let them take some extra shots.

■ Chris Lawler is asleep in the basement bedroom of his parent's house on Beach 131st Street. He should be in class right now, at St. John's University Law School. His mother, Kathie, is on the phone. His dad, Tom, is taking advantage of a mild November morning by getting in a round of golf. His two sisters, Katelyn and Jennifer, are at basketball practice at Bishop Kearney High School in Brooklyn. His brother, Brendan, is away at college.

■ Flip Mullen is at home. He hears what he thinks must be the Concorde. He'd just read that they were resuming flights and, dear God, isn't that a racket! He doesn't remember it ever being *that* loud.

■ Tom Lynch, a retired firefighter, is on Rockaway Beach Boule-vard taking his regular morning exercise march. He watches an airplane complete a banked turn and start towards the ocean. *Holy shit.* He sees a small explosion in the fuselage behind the wing.

Two more seconds elapse and suddenly there's a second explosion, engulfing most of the plane in flames.

■ A large American flag is stretched neatly along a cyclone fence outside the Young Israel School of Belle Harbor on Beach 129th Street and Cronston Avenue. George Deligiannis is on his way to the coffee shop when he pulls to a stop sign across from the school. The flag looks nice there; the bright blue sky is a perfect backdrop.

His eyes widen as an American Airlines plane soars into view. A puff of smoke pops out of the side of the plane, like a clay pigeon at a skeet shoot. The tail of the plane separates; it seems to hang in the air for a moment before it starts to fall like a piece of loose-leaf paper.

■ Pete Hayden sees an explosion on the right side of the plane, behind the wing. The plane starts to come apart. He's watching it the whole way. It starts sliding to the side and flips a bit, so that it appears almost cross-like in the sky. Then it turns again and starts to nose-dive.

■ Jimmy Bulloch is in the office of his Texaco service station, which sits in the middle of the one-block commercial strip of Beach 129th Street. It's been in the family for decades. The Bullochs owned the place when the 1966 Christmas fire killed the three Daly kids, who lived right next door. Jimmy is having his morning coffee, mindlessly keeping an eye on the fuel truck filling the underground tanks.

■ Maureen Edwards is at her kitchen sink, rinsing the bowls the kids used for their morning cereal. Something catches her eye out the window. She screams when she sees the fiery plane falling like a huge flaming arrow . . . diving . . . *where is it going to hit?*

■ The three kids—Alex, Mike, and Mark—look up because of a loud noise. A plane is heading straight down, corkscrewing, twirling like a helicopter's rotors. It looks like it might hit the church. They bolt towards the schoolyard across the street.

■ Matt Tansey is incorporating the sound outside into his dream—a dream of a plane crashing. His girlfriend screams. He's out of his sleep now, pulling aside the blinds on the window.

■ American Airlines Flight 587 slams into Belle Harbor on Beach 131st Street.

■ An enormous boom rocks St. Francis de Sales Church. Stunned, Monsignor Geraghty says, "I don't know what that was, but it's time to go find your loved ones and get safe."

■ Jimmy Bulloch, a big man, is thrown backwards and falls to the floor. Luckily, the windows of his Texaco gas station are blown outwards. He thinks a car has exploded.

■ A chunk of steel crashes through the bedroom window of Ray and Linda Marten, two doors down from the Harbor Light and just around the corner from the service station. Linda and the kids had been there just a minute before.

■ Pete Hayden sees the bulk of the plane nose-dive into the neighborhood, and a ball of fire that looks 20 stories high blooms over the houses. He runs to his house, grabs the phone, and calls his wife, Rita.

"There's another terrorist attack. A plane just went down. I'm okay, but I'm going to help."

■ Bernie Heeran feels his house shake. He lives just a couple of houses off a corner where a thousand car accidents have happened over the years. For most of them, he'd be the first one on the scene. He thinks two trucks must've collided.

Then his brother-in-law, who lives just next door, starts pounding on the door. He's screaming something about Rockaway being

bombed. Bernie, barefoot, is trying to make sense of what he's saying, when he looks across the street to Bulloch's service station
and sees something on fire.

He throws on a pair of docksider shoes and runs towards Bulloch's. He doesn't know what he's looking at—though, he says to
himself, it's not a car. At the same time, he wishes he were wearing a belt. He's lost weight since Charlie was killed and now it
feels like his pants are going to fall off.

He runs into Bulloch's storefront, grabs a fire extinguisher, and
empties it on what he now realizes is a burning jet engine. He then
grabs a garden hose that shoots water, then stops, shoots some
more, and then stops again. There's a knot in the line somewhere.

Bulloch says, "You'd better go to the Harbor Light," as he frees
the hose and grabs it.

Until then, Bernie had no idea the plane itself had crashed just
around the corner. In the sky, he looks up at a massive ball of fire
and smoke. He thinks of his sister who is supposed to be in the
Harbor Light. She had opened up the place that morning.

■ McVeigh is on the phone with his wife, Pat, just checking in.

Pat says, "Hold on. You won't believe the wind that just shook
the house."

He says, "I gotta go. A call's just come in."

■ Tommy Carroll is driving east, passing Beach 112th Street, when
he sees a driver in another car going west suddenly flinch. *What
was that about?* He looks in his rear-view mirror and sees a black
cloud growing over Belle Harbor. He thinks it might be a gas
explosion. He wonders how close it is to his house—where he left
the girls.

■ Steve Stathis, in his blue-and-white company car, turns onto
Newport Avenue at Beach 116th Street and is jolted back in his
seat. Fire and black smoke plume over the houses somewhere
down Newport. The oxygen overhead draws the fire like an
orange popcorn ball to the sky. He doesn't know what to think

and presses on the accelerator. He has to swerve as people run out of their houses and into the street for a look. The car window is open, so he's able to hear someone say something about a plane crashing.

Among the first to arrive, he parks his car and bangs on the doors of nearby houses, making certain no one is in the corner homes across from the inferno. Years of training at Con Ed compel his eyes to check the overhead wires and a pole-mounted transformer. They're on fire. He shouts for everyone to keep away, wondering where the hell the fire engines are. He could hear them coming, just a second ago; now where are they? A man, apparently in shock, walks aimlessly under the burning wires until Steve grabs him by the shoulders and steers him away.

An off-duty firefighter, Jim Sherwood, says to get ready, all available hands would be needed to offload hoses as soon as an engine arrives. Steve's glad Sherwood's among those here to help. He knows what he's doing. Sherwood saved some kids when the World Trade Center was bombed in 1993.

■ Bernie Heeran has a split second of relief when he sees that the Harbor Light has been spared, which means his sister is okay. Now he's got to see what he can do to help.

■ There's too much fire and black smoke to discern much of anything. There's no sign of the plane. What can be seen are some of the houses, fully intact, with curtains of flame, three stories high, shrouding them. The radiant heat is fierce. Your eyes dry and the rims of your ears pick up the heat from 100 feet away.

■ Normally, Engine 268 from Beach 116th Street would be the first on the scene at Beach 131st Street. However, as 268 races down Newport Avenue, they're pointed to a burning house on Beach 128th Street, three blocks short of the real conflagration.

With Engine 268 turning to fight the fire on Beach 128th Street, the truck, Ladder 137, from the Beach 116th Street firehouse sails ahead towards the black smoke three short blocks ahead. The truck screeches to a stop and Lieutenant Billy Gallagher hops out. The fire's really roaring; at a minimum, he knows four corner houses are fully involved, yet there's frustratingly little to do until an engine arrives with its hoses. He instructs his chauffeur where to place the rig and then tells his men to make primary searches as best they can.

∎ The black smoke rises, covering the sky above. The sun shrinks and fades the way it does during a solar eclipse. Overhead wires—who knew there were so many?—are flaming and smoking against the darkening sky.

The wind—always the damn Rockaway wind in these fires—blows some heat and embers towards the bay and nearby homes.

Engine 329 from the usually sleepy firehouse near Fort Tilden flies down Newport Avenue from the west end. Steve Stathis joins with firefighters, on duty and off duty, and begins to frantically stretch line. He sees Bernie Heeran charge up Newport Avenue towards Beach 131st Street, barking out orders, heading into the wall of fire.

Firefighters quickly hook the hoses to the hydrant, and Steve and others run the lines close to the flames. Close to hell, because that's what it looks like. Minutes ago, it was a beautiful Monday morning in Belle Harbor. Now he's holding a hose next to friends, Turtle McManus and Tom O'Connor, wondering if this fire will ever be controlled.

∎ Again, Matt Tansey lets adrenaline and a hero's reflex take over. He drives his girlfriend to a friend's house a mile away, barely stops the car to let her out, then flies back to the crash site. In front of the Harbor Light, not feeling his neck or back, he grabs a length of hose and helps run it towards the house on fire across the street.

∎ Whipper Stathis is called to the phone at his firehouse. Eileen, his wife, calling from work, yells into the phone that a plane just crashed in Belle Harbor. She's crying. People are dead. He pleads with her to calm down and get home to the kids. He's on his way, too.

■ Ronnie Darcy, a Rockaway guy working with George Johnson at Ladder 15 in Manhattan, hears the FDNY voice alarm in quarters and shouts, "That's a Rockaway box!" The box number signifies where the call came in from—whether it's by phone or an alarm pull-box on a street corner. He calls his wife at home and then yells, "A plane just crashed in Rockaway!"

The firefighters turn on the TV. It looks like the entire neighborhood is on fire. The dispatcher starts banging out a fifth alarm for Beach 128th Street and Newport Avenue; then a seventh alarm for Beach 129th and Beach 131st Street. George hears something about Beach 129th Street—where his girlfriend and her family live. He calls and gets nothing but busy signals.

■ Monsignor Geraghty removes items from the altar, goes into the sacristy, and removes his vestments. He leaves the church through a side door that faces the backs of homes of Beach 130th Street. The fire is massive and high, and seems close enough that Geraghty thinks the houses right before him are aflame. He is immediately struck by how loud the fire is. Popping sounds, one after another. Geraghty fears the entire block must be on fire. The popping sounds must be from furnaces in the houses or gas lines. How long will it take before this fire is brought under control?

He works his way down Beach 130th Street, closer to the fire he now sees stems from another block over, Beach 131st Street. Some people, scared and shocked, are running past him; others run towards the fire. He offers a blessing, a general absolution amid the confusion. As he nears the corner, he sees Bernie Heeran and others rushing ever closer to the fire. He is struck by their bravery. The fire—its heat, its angry sounds—is terrifying.

Civilians and off-duty firefighters are warning people to get away. Others are running up to houses, banging on doors, or opening the doors and calling inside, warning everyone to get out.

■ A woman, screaming, runs away from the fire on Beach 131st Street. Black, black smoke rolls up the street behind her.

■ Peter Brady and Billy Collins, in a "terrorism response" class on Staten Island, hear the news and bolt towards their cars.

■ Kenny Whelan, on the FDR Drive, gets a call from his sister, Elaine, on his cell phone. "A plane has crashed. I'm not sure where because I can't see up the block with all the smoke."

As soon as he turns on the car radio, he hears a reporter say an American Airlines jet has crashed in Belle Harbor at Beach 129th Street and Newport Avenue—which happens to be exactly where his condominium apartment is—and where he left his 23-year-old son, Ryan, asleep.

■ The stock market will open in about 10 minutes. Billy Heeran hears something about a plane crashing; he thinks he's heard them say it crashed into the Marine Park Bridge. He looks up at one of the TV screens and sees a map of Rockaway. There's an arrow pointing to Belle Harbor, to Beach 129th Street. He feels a jolt in his heart and stomach. *Shit, no.* He can't believe it—an arrow on the TV screen, pointing right at his house.

He can't get through to his father—or anybody else in Rockaway. Normally carefree and easy going, he's now frantic, unsure what the hell to do. Somebody tells him to calm down and he says, "Calm down? Don't tell me to calm down. That's where my family lives."

He calls his brother, Sean. They've got to get to Rockaway.

■ Tommy Carroll flies into his house, barks at the two girls in their pajamas—daughter Brianne and cousin Patrice—to get in the car. He's going to drop them off 3 miles west at his brother's house in Breezy Point, figuring it's going to be a long day. He drives 90 MPH on the way there. Sean, Tommy's six-year-old, is mildly amused by the wild ride; the girls, unnerved, sit in silence.

■ Kevin Lunny, now in bunker gear, which he keeps in the trunk of his car, is hurrying along Newport Avenue. He sees a handful of civilians standing in front of the Harbor Light near a car, an official's sedan, parked at the hydrant.

"Move that car," Lunny says.

The civilians just shrug, collectively saying, "It's not ours."

Lunny, who's still moving towards the fire, yells, *"Move that fuckin' car!"*

The eight or 10 civilians quickly look at each other, then go to the car. They bend, then lift, carry, and push the car away from the hydrant.

■ Palmer Doyle bolts from his house, runs five blocks, then joins others fighting the fire on Beach 128th Street. He shouts to a couple of friends, civilians, "Come on! Lend a hand. Grab the hoses. Stretch that line, and run 'em through the gate, up the steps and into the house. *Hurry!*"

He leaps over a cyclone fence to assess what's going on at the rear of the house, and is suddenly puzzled by the sight of this hulking piece of steel in the backyard of the big house. Holy shit, it's a jet's engine!

A civilian says, "There's a fucking inferno on 131st. The whole block."

■ Whipper Stathis is the chauffeur at Ladder 173, so no one has to tell him to speed up as he moves the truck along Cross Bay Boulevard through Broad Channel, then over the Cross Bay Bridge into Rockaway. The lieutenant in the truck tells Whipper to slow down.

Whipper hands him his phone and asks him to call his wife. The lieutenant says slow down. Whipper presses on the accelerator and says, *"Just fuckin' call my wife!"*

As they cross the water, to his right he can see pockets of fire in addition to the huge funnel coming from Beach 131st Street. He thinks Rockaway is under attack. They're shooting missiles at us.

He has one of those sudden thoughts. Was summer that long ago? Surfing and barbecues. Now we're under attack.

People across Rockaway immediately think another plane or more will strike. Some hear just the explosion and think bombs are being dropped. This isn't just a plane crash—*it's an attack.* Because of Mike Moran, what he did at the concert, he had to say that he was from Rockaway. He had to say, "Kiss my ass, Osama, you bitch."

Some people grab their kids, jump in their cars, and head towards Brooklyn. They drive with their necks stretched, trying to see upward through their windshield, trying to see if bombs or planes are falling.

■ Gerry Davan, an off-duty FDNY lieutenant, bolts from his house four blocks from the crash. When he arrives on the scene, four houses on the southeast side of Beach 131st Street are fully involved, their flames threatening to consume the rest of the block. He grabs a length of hose and repositions it, so it's between the last house on fire and the next one not yet aflame. He is without a helmet or gear, and can feel the hot smoke on his exposed skin.

Jimmy Cashin—another firefighter and off duty as well—works the nozzle, spraying, both of them hoping they've got enough lines to fight a jet fuel fire.

■ Kenny Whelan yanks the steering wheel of his car, cuts across three lanes on the FDR Drive, exits, swings wide of cars at a red light, and dodges oncoming traffic. The Volvo speeds across the 59th Street Bridge into Queens. Construction is underway, and traffic cones point traffic away from Queens Boulevard where he needs to go. His wife and mother are screaming at him to slow down. He screams even louder, telling them to shut up! *That* quiets things for a moment. He's thinking the worst. Ryan is dead. He knocks over a traffic cone and winds his way through barriers trying to get to Queens Boulevard.

As soon as he's clear and ready to fly down the boulevard, a police cruiser with lights flashing appears in his rear-view mirror. Kenny pulls to the side, feeling like a madman. He identifies himself as a captain with the fire department, and tells the cop he thinks his house has been hit by the plane.

The cop goes back to the cruiser, radios headquarters, then comes back. "Let's go. Follow me."

■ On Beach 128th Street, the multifamily house is on fire, with maybe five or six apartments. It's hard to know if everyone is accounted for. The fire runs along the roof, the top floor, and the back of the house. The garage is on fire as well as the pleasure boat, which is resting on cinder blocks and planks in front of the garage and next to the fallen jet engine. The siding on the house next door starts to melt.

Some off-duty firefighters are doing what they can. They might not know each other's names, but each can recognize another firefighter. You hear, "Brother, we need a line around the back" and "Brother, we got any foam to put on the boat?" and "Brother, gimme a hand with this."

■ Palmer Doyle climbs atop a minivan parked in the alley, just ahead of the boat, and grabs the nozzle from a civilian, Bobby O'Hara. Doyle's worried the fuel on the boat might ignite. On the third floor of the house, firefighters from Engine 268 have worked themselves inside. They ventilate the fire by knocking out windows—a shower of glass rains down on O'Hara and Doyle.

■ In Manhattan, George Johnson can't reach Rockaway by phone. He looks at the captain. "Cap, I gotta go."

The captain shakes his head. "You can't leave." The captain wasn't being officious or hard-hearted; he simply can't be sure if the plane crash is an isolated incident or if another round of terrorism is underway.

George doesn't care about other concerns at this point. "Cap, my girlfriend lives on that block. I'm leaving."

As they go back and forth, the captain turns to a firefighter who had worked the night shift and was now leaving for home, and asks if he can cover. The firefighter hesitates. The captain shouts, *"Yes or no?"*

The guy shrugs, okay. The captain looks at George. "Take off."

George doesn't have his car at the firehouse, but Jim Cavanaugh says, "Catch," and tosses him his car keys. He throws his gear in the back of the car and starts pulling out, when all the firefighters come out of the firehouse screaming for him to wait.

"The troopers will take you!"

A state trooper's car screeches to a halt. George throws his gear in the trunk and they take off, tires spinning for a second before gripping the road. As they leave the Battery Tunnel, the troopers get a call on their radio telling them to go and close off some street in Manhattan. It looks like terrorism; there has to be an immediate lockdown.

One of the troopers takes the radio and explains they are transporting a firefighter to Rockaway. No good, turn around. A supervisor orders them to get back to Manhattan.

They're on the Belt Parkway now, just under the Verrazano Narrows Bridge, another 10 miles to Rockaway. The troopers are getting a lot of flak. They exchange looks. George worries they're going to drop him right here and head back to Manhattan. He'll be stuck on the side of the road.

He's desperate to get to Rockaway. He's got to play the only card he has. "Listen. I don't know if it'll do you guys any good, but if you catch a lot of heat when you get back to Manhattan, you know that picture with the three firefighters raising the flag over the rubble at Ground Zero?" George pauses as the driver glances at him in the rear-view mirror. "I'm, uh, one of those guys."

The driver, forgetting about the road for a moment, turns around and presents his hand to George to shake it. "I'm a Marine. That picture is plastered all over my house." The driver smiles, turns back, and presses the pedal. The state trooper car flies along the Belt Parkway at better than a 100 MPH. George knows he's getting home—in a hurry.

It so happens that even flying in a state trooper's car won't get George there any sooner than his father, George, Sr., who bolted out of his house when he saw the Hiroshima-like fire cloud rise above the houses. George, Sr. had spent 32 years with the FDNY. It's the kind of experience that makes you run 10 blocks in loose-fitting shoes to help.

■ On Beach 131st Street, Steve Stathis thinks about jet fuel. Everybody's heard so much about jet fuel since September 11. What's it going to do here? Burn everything from bay to ocean? All these guys in street clothes know what they're doing. They're all off-duty firefighters and cops, and a lot of civilians are here, waiting for orders. They'll do what they can.

He catches a glimpse of someone climbing into the passenger side of Engine 329. Suddenly, he feels a whole lot better. That's Pete Hayden, the deputy chief himself. He looks like a civilian in his khaki pants, but there's no doubt: he's in charge. Then Steve sees a top EMS guy, Andy McCraken. That guy knows what he's doing, too.

■ In the cab of Engine 329, Pete Hayden gets on the radio and tells the dispatcher what is going on and what is needed. He lets the dispatcher know that he'd be the one in charge. Although he is not in uniform, Chief Hayden—a long-time Rockaway guy—is known by most of the dozens of firefighters, both on- and off-duty firefighters already on the scene, so they take directions from him without hesitation. He makes sure a perimeter building search is done and the houses so marked.

Evacuate the houses. Stretch those lines. Surround the fire!

■ Palmer Doyle on Beach 128th Street is hosing the burning boat in the alley. Volunteers from the Broad Channel Volunteer Fire Department arrive to help—and it's a good thing. Most first responders shot directly to Beach 131st Street.

■ Flip Mullen is on Beach 131st. "Jesus Christ, I've been here on a job before." He doesn't know whose house it is, but that's where he "saved" a German shepherd named Whiskey. There'll be no jokes this time around.

■ A stream of off-duty guys and many on their way to funerals rush into the Beach 116th Street firehouse, stripping it of firefighter gear and equipment. After grabbing what they can, most of them hop in their cars and get as close as they can to the scene; others run the whole way to Beach 131st Street.

■ Retired firefighter Bernie Heeran is shouting at others to hurry and send the line over the fence.

■ Besides the three mostly demolished homes, five others in the vicinity of the corner of Beach 131st Street catch fire after getting spritzed with jet fuel. However, if there is good news, it's that the fires are exterior blazes, with most of the flames confined to the outside walls of the homes. Such fires can be extinguished with relative ease, assuming firefighters get to them in quick fashion. Once a fire gets inside, it's much more uncertain and dangerous. Brick houses can heat like ovens or act like chimneys, though the exterior can appear rather preserved. Yet, no matter if the house is frame or brick, once a fire gets going inside, structural risks and hidden dangers come into play. That's not a concern now. With all the firefighters here, water is on the houses in a hurry.

Another break comes with the wind—or lack of it. It seems like there is always wind in Rockaway, but now the air is still.

■ After dropping the kids in Breezy Point, Tommy Carroll shoots back, parks the car as close as he can, then runs to the scene. He feels like a Johnny-come-lately because so many firefighters are already here—and, damn, they've done some job! The fire is just about out. Maybe 329, near Fort Tilden, is not the busiest house in the FDNY, but the guys really stepped up; they were ready when needed.

■ Three blocks east, the fires were out. The fires on the roof of the garage and the boat in the alley had been a little stubborn, but they didn't spread. Now firefighters and volunteers were just hosing the house and garage to keep the fire from reigniting.

■ The police cruiser just in front of Kenny Whelan speeds over the Cross Bay Bridge. Kenny sees white smoke billowing skyward from the crash site. White smoke is a good sign. He doesn't know what's happened or who's been hurt, but, unbelievably, the white smoke suggests the fire or fires are under control, perhaps extinguished.

On the Rockaway side, the roadway splits—one side towards Far Rockaway; the other towards Belle Harbor. The cop, unfamiliar with Rockaway, goes left. Kenny doesn't need an escort from here. He goes right, flying down the off ramp towards Belle Harbor.

His wife and mother scream at him again to slow down, he's going to get everybody killed. Here we go again. Shut up! *Please* shut up! His son Ryan is dead. He knows it. Ryan is dead.

■ Once the smoke clears, the burned bodies from the plane emerge. Some are still strapped in seats. Many are strewn about the street and some are on top of the rubble, which, an hour ago, were three handsome homes. The corpse of a man, burned badly, is a few yards off to the side. He's holding an infant tight to his chest. It looks as if the child is fused to the father.

Tommy Carroll, Chief Hayden, Flip Mullen, Whipper Stathis—and so many others who were engulfed in dust, debris, and death at the World Trade Center—now find themselves surrounded by more than 250 bodies. Two hundred and fifty dead bodies might as well be a thousand. The poor souls are everywhere. There is some evidence of who these passengers were —some luggage here and there, a child's toy.

There's no standing around, just staring. Everyone—and there are a couple hundred people—is fast at work. It's an ant hill of navy blue shirts and black and yellow bunker gear. Crash victims are secured in body bags; debris is moved.

Some firefighters begin a desperate dig, always hoping to find someone alive, even if there is simply no chance.

■ Wild-eyed, Kenny parks at Beach 124th Street and runs three blocks until he's stopped by a young woman, Amber Farrell. "It's not your house. *It's not your house!*"

That's good, but where is Ryan? Kenny starts running again, and then he sees his 23-year-old boy standing casually at the corner. Kenny grabs him, hugs him, slobbers all over him about how much he loves him.

Ryan, not knowing that his father had reason to be so concerned, looks slightly amused. "Dad, relax." Kenny's still choked up. "Dad, take it easy!"

■ George Johnson directs the state troopers to the last stretch of this 13-mile race from the city, down Rockaway Beach Boulevard as far as they can go, before emergency vehicles clog the streets. George jumps out, grabs all of his gear from the trunk, shakes their hands, and starts running for his girlfriend's house. When you're in a desperate hurry, the gear can feel like you're carrying a safe. After two or three blocks, he sees a friend standing on her front lawn. George rips off his gear, asks her to keep an eye on it, and starts running again.

While passing houses and blocks where so many friends live, George begins clicking them off in his head. Okay, they're okay. They're okay. He's okay. Thank God, they're okay.

Sucking wind, still running as hard as he can, George turns down his girlfriend's block and sees that the block and her house are untouched. Still, he crashes through the front door and everyone in the house comes running. They whoop and holler when they see George, then try to ask where he had come from and how he got there.

However, George has the first question. "You're all okay?"

They give him quick assurance, but seem more concerned with how he's doing as he's still huffing and puffing. "Where'd you run from?"

"Manhattan." That makes everyone pause. "Well, I mean I actually ran about six blocks."

■ Billy and Sean Heeran run down the stairs to the subway. It's the only way out of Manhattan. Billy's car is parked in Brooklyn. They'll grab the car and get to Rockaway somehow.

CHAPTER 7

Silver Linings

November 2001

Mayor Giuliani stands on the corner of Beach 129th Street and Rockaway Beach Boulevard, just off the steps of St. Francis de Sales Church. He'd been here more than 10 times in the last two months to attend wakes, funerals, and memorials. Sometimes he would speak; sometimes he would just be another mourner. The 48 hours or so after the attacks of September 11 had forever changed his legacy. He became a phenomenon on the world stage. He was at once gritty, brave, compassionate, defiant, and reassuring. He was tireless and visible. He seemed to assume leadership without grabbing it. He led without bully or bluster.

A few contrarians said any mayor or leader would have done the same. The fact is that most New Yorkers—even his growing legion of critics who eagerly looked forward to the end of his administration—acknowledged his deft hand in the crisis. Few New York mayors leave office loved or revered. The events of September 11 made Giuliani a superstar. Crowds at ball games, rallies, or out-of-town events showered him with raucous praise.

His presence in Rockaway, however, is sadly routine. It coincides with bagpipes, tears, and coffins. He comes; he goes. Invariably, it's too sad an occasion to applaud him or even give him a second thought. People fill the church and line the sidewalk outside to say good-bye to family members or friends—not to catch a glimpse of Mayor Giuliani.

Yet, today, it's different. He's here because it's a disaster. The air smells of jet fuel and burnt flesh. They're calling it Ground Zero II.

Giuliani, in his navy blue windbreaker, briefing reporters about a disaster around the corner, seems as odd a sight as the aircraft carrier stationed off Rockaway Beach a couple of months before. It's another example of life being turned upside down in the beachfront neighborhood. He's become a familiar sight at funerals, but now he's holding a press conference about a plane crash a few hundred yards away. It can't be.

As he provides reporters with preliminary news about the crash, black smoke wafts out of a storm drain across the street. Apparently, a blast of black smoke at the crash site had shot into the sewer system and was now spewing out three blocks away. People keep their distance; they don't know if it's jet fuel that might suddenly ignite and blow manhole covers into the air.

■ Once the fire is knocked down on Beach 128th Street, Palmer Doyle heads to Beach 131st Street, knowing Engine 268 and the Broad Channel Vollies would make sure the fire didn't reignite here. He's heard that most of the plane came down just three blocks over and it was hell over there.

Doyle weaves his way through a mass of emergency responders. He glances at the Harbor Light on the corner of Beach 130th Street—untouched. Right across the street, on the east corner, firefighters are hosing a house badly damaged by fire. He just has to take a few more steps before he sees the house directly behind it, on the corner of Beach 131st Street, burned out as well.

Across the street, on the south side of Newport Avenue, there's a huge chunk of fuselage. The homes that were here are now a pile of smoldering rubble. Still, he's struck at how confined the area of devastation is. A house on the corner of Beach 130th Street, diagonally across from the Harbor Light and directly behind where most of the fuselage lay, no more than a basketball shot away, is completely untouched.

He sees McVeigh, McCormack, and so many others from the neighborhood putting bodies in bags. He goes to join them. It's ugly déjà vu—just a few weeks back, he was doing the same thing at Ground Zero.

■ Monsignor Geraghty opens the school building and gym so that various agencies—Secret Service, NYPD, FBI, National Transportation Safety Board (NTSB), and others—can establish their command posts. He even provides access to a supply closet so agencies can use magic markers, crayons, and tape to post signs such as "FBI."

They have to move the bodies somewhere. Someone suggests the gymnasium of St. Francis de Sales School. Tarps are spread out across the gym floor.

"Whoa, whoa, wait a minute," Pete Hayden tells the Office of Emergency Management. "That's not such a good idea. There has been enough tragedy around here, enough bad memories. This is a school; kids will be using this gym. It shouldn't be used as a morgue."

The officials pause but are not swayed. It seems like Hayden might be overruled until an official says Floyd Bennett Field might be a better place. It's bigger than the St. Francis gym. Floyd Bennett, once a commercial and military airfield, is just a few minutes away. Bodies can be put in the old hangars that still remain.

■ In the car, Billy and Sean Heeran are stopped while trying to get onto the Belt Parkway, but are allowed through after telling the cop that they think their house has been hit by the plane. As they speed towards Rockaway, Billy calls a friend on his cell phone, and learns his family and the Harbor Light have been spared, but the Lawler's house has been hit. It's at once a relief and a nightmare. The Lawlers are like family, too. Chris Lawler is a great friend—an RIB.

■ Monsignor Geraghty makes the "small hall" at St. Francis available to officials as a communications and command center. Within an hour, 50 phone lines are operating out of this impromptu emergency headquarters. On his way to the rectory, he sees three firefighters coming from the crash site, looking grim. He lightens the mood, even if it's just for a moment.

"You guys get dressed up for fires, huh?"

They look down at themselves and smile. It seems they had forgotten what they were wearing. Just a few hours before, they had been driving to a memorial on Long Island, and raced to Rockaway instead when they heard the news on the radio. They had stopped at the firehouse on Beach 116th Street and grabbed helmets and turnout coats—and tossed them over their dress clothes.

"Only when we come to Rockaway, Father."

■ Billy and Sean Heeran see some Rockaway friends on the side of the road, trying to get to Rockaway on foot. They tell them to get in, and then plead their case to an officer at the entrance of the Marine Park Bridge. Although they're allowed over the bridge to Rockaway, that's as far as they're allowed to go. Police are everywhere.

They park the car at the firehouse, just steps off the bridge, next to Fort Tilden, and head to the beach. They'll run along the shore, to avoid all the police barricades, from Beach 169th Street to Beach 131st Street. One way or the other, they're getting home.

■ Word gets out fast that the Lawler's house was hit. Kathie Lawler was on the phone with her sister, Ann Marie Greene. Both women are from the Blum family. Everyone knows the Blums or someone married to a Blum. They're fourth generation Rockaway. The family is sprinkled throughout the neighborhood. If you want to find one of them, you can check the beach at 133rd Street. If it's a nice summer day on the weekend, the Blums will have staked out a big spot on the sand.

They have five firefighters in the family. Since September 11, they've counted themselves among the lucky because none were killed that day. The good fortune stretches to another member of the family, Kevin Blum, as well. Kevin worked in the World Financial Center but was away on business that day. Like the firefighters in the family, he's been called a hero, too. In 1993, he was one of the people who tackled Colin Ferguson, the madman who opened fire with automatic weapons on a crowded Long Island Railroad car, shooting 25 people and killing six. More might have been shot had Blum and another passenger not pounced on Ferguson when he paused to reload.

Today, good fortune is mixed with tragedy. Firefighters are digging through rubble, looking for mother and son, Kathie and Chris Lawler. The guys digging are more than firefighters; they're family and friends. Walter Blum and Peter Blum, Donnie Olsen, and Larry Gray are all among those searching. Kenny Whelan's there, too. They're trying to get to the basement where they believe Chris was sleeping. Eventually, they do find Chris in his bed. Kenny is struck by how peaceful he seems, and it looks like he just got his hair cut. Maybe he'll tell Tom Lawler about that. Maybe it'll make him feel better.

■ The crash of a major airline jet always attracts great media attention, but now, because of the possibility of terrorism, the interest is extreme. *The Wave* Web site gets 84,000 unique visitor hits; most days, it'll get fewer than 1,500.

The phones are either out of service or overloaded. Families and friends can't get through. In the Arverne fire of 1922, residents—most of whom didn't have phones—relied on local phone operators to relay messages to others. Residents had a choice of waiting endlessly for an available phone at a nearby hotel or shop, or they could walk a mile or so to the telephone building and ask that operators send messages across the city and country (usually to other operators because household phones were uncommon in most areas). Now, kids in the neighborhood let family and friends from the outside world know they're okay by Instant Message and e-mail.

■ Streets surrounding the site, and even a half-mile away, are closed by police. At some corners, they let you pass on foot; on others, you had better have a damn good reason to get past. It's a Swiss cheese lockdown. The cops can't seem to decide if they should stop the kids on bikes who want to get close to the scene, or all these people who might be relatives and close friends of the people who were killed.

The Red Cross sets up at the Harbor Light—just as it had 35 years before when the Christmas fire of 1966 killed the Daly kids, when the place was called the Newport Inn.

There's nothing festive, but the crowds make the streets look like there's a big block party going on. Fire trucks and engines line Newport Avenue and Rockaway Beach Boulevard. Television trucks and their extended antennae are parked on every corner.

People everywhere are hugging each other. Some who've probably never exchanged more than a polite hello are now laughing and crying in each other's arms. Preteen kids in groups enjoy the spectacle. To be sure, some kids were shaken up, even traumatized, but some of the kids think it's cool. They give interviews—some really want to get on television—and plenty chat with police and firefighters.

People stand in clusters along the avenues, recalling where they were when the plane crashed, trying to get news about how many people are dead. Some remark that the acoustics varied from block to block, even house to house. Some heard no noise but felt their houses shake. Some heard the plane's engine groaning, struggling. Others heard a roar similar to the Concorde. Others only heard the impact and subsequent explosions.

An odd, collective mood is in the air, reminiscent—but not the same—of a blackout or heavy snowstorm, where everyone in the neighborhood has the same experience at the same time. Now, a few thousand people feel as if they've just escaped death. It's a familiar, but not common, feeling.

How often does sudden death skim past someone in the course of a normal life? A tractor-trailer cuts you off on the highway; a big wave buries you; you take a misstep on a high ladder. You feel your heart drop or stop. Your insides tell you that was one close call. You're too stunned to be happy. You're relieved but, damn, things sure could've changed in that instant. Although you're stunned, your senses are heightened. You're suddenly more aware; you take steps to be more careful, or prepare yourself for another tractor-trailer or wave. You're roused but alive—in a sense more alive than you were seconds before. You're grateful.

So, if others were in the car with you when you had a close call, you all share the same feelings. Now, an entire neighborhood is full of people nodding at each other, all sharing those feelings that come with a very close call.

■ Some firefighters walk away from the site in tears. Some say it was worse than Ground Zero—worse than anything they saw on September 11. Some can barely talk through heaving sobs. Burned bodies everywhere. Not only that, the bodies are strewn on a block they know. Right over there is the Harbor Light, the neighborhood pub. What's the Red Cross doing there? *This is home.*

At Ground Zero, it was mostly dust. Body parts, sure, but that's easier in a way. At Ground Zero, you didn't see a father holding his baby. These people knew they were going to crash. People at the Twin Towers probably were killed before they knew what was happening. Someone else says that it's all a matter of perspective.

The recovery continues at the site; bodies are being carried away. Workers in white protective suits tread cautiously over the rubble of destroyed homes.

Television reports note that it was an American Airlines flight heading for the Dominican Republic that crashed at 9:17 this morning. It is learned that many of the people on board were returning home, and many others lived in Washington Heights in Manhattan and were traveling to visit family still residing on the island country in the Caribbean.

■ It is odd, unsettling, and perhaps wrong to call something a miracle when 265 people are killed by a plane crash. There is certainly no miracle for the people on board Flight 587 or their families. There is no miracle for the victims and families on the ground. Yet, it seems like a miracle or crazy-ass luck to a few thousand people in Belle Harbor.

A plane crashes nearly dead center of the Rockaway peninsula and all the ingredients of a holocaust are in place: jet fuel, high winds, houses side by side, a fallen jet engine smoldering at a service station, another engine igniting a house around the corner, and a bridge under construction that will surely impede rescue vehicles. (The Marine Park Bridge had been undergoing a major rehab job. Incoming traffic was limited to a single, very narrow lane.)

Some call it the fire that didn't happen. A lot of the jet fuel was spilled over Jamaica Bay as the plane started to break up. One jet engine smashed into a service station, just feet from the gas tanks and inches from a gasoline refilling truck. Had it happened just a few feet in the other direction, catastrophic explosions would likely have occurred. The bulk of the other engine skimmed the back of a house and landed in the backyard, rather than smack in the middle of the house or on some other vulnerable spot nearby. The inhabitants were tossed across rooms from the impact, but all escaped without harm. The fire at this location, including the boat in the alleyway, caused by the hot and flaming engine, was relatively small and could be fought by a limited number of people.

The wind, an accomplice in so many devastating blazes in Rockaway's past, suddenly let up.

The plane nose-dived. Had the plane skidded or plowed its way through the neighborhood, one home after another would have been destroyed.

St. Francis School was closed for Veteran's Day. Although the school narrowly escaped harm, had the school been in session, the students (and the teachers, for that matter) would have been terrified and traumatized by the sound overhead and the inferno just outside the school windows. Most parents, at this early part of the day, knew exactly where their kids were. Had there been school, parents would have gone to work or the store, or simply gone back home after dropping the kids off at school. If the plane crash had occurred on a school day, the parents of 800 kids would have rushed to St. Francis, just a block from the site. For many, it would have been a desperate, hysterical trip from Manhattan or elsewhere. Baby-sitters work just fine most days, but when a plane crashes near your kids' school, you don't wait for news on the phone or television.

▪ Kenny Whelan, a captain with the fire department, was able to get a police escort from Manhattan to Rockaway. He was fortunate that he had his FDNY shield in the car and had been stopped by an understanding cop. With the immediate security lockdown that occurred, you can bet many parents would have been delayed or even prevented from getting to Rockaway.

Another critical factor in limiting the devastation was the rapid response of off-duty and retired firefighters who were on the scene in seconds. Had the crash happened in another neighborhood, it's possible that many residents would have rushed to help.

In Rockaway—which some have called Home of the Bravest because so many firefighters live there—many of the residents are not only willing to help, they're quite able and ready to help. When the engines with their hoses arrived, the off-duty and retired guys didn't have to wait to be told what to do. Hose was coming off the truck before it came to a complete stop. In seconds, the hydrant was feeding four lines. Uniformed, off-duty firefighters and civilians stretched the lines and surrounded the fires.

Because of the local response and the quick flood of emergency responders who came by the Cross Bay Bridge, it didn't much matter that the Marine Park Bridge—one of the two bridges to Rockaway—was under construction.

Even among the devastated homes, the loss of life could have been greater. Two of the people who died were a married couple in their 70's; none of their five children or 14 grandchildren were visiting that day. Four of the six people who lived next door were already out of the house for the day. Two doors down, two of the three people inside escaped with their lives.

American Airlines Flight 587 was an Airbus A-300, a plane big enough to be classified as a "heavy" in the parlance of air traffic control. More than 177 feet in length, the wide-bodied airliner had a wingspan of 147 feet. The top of an Airbus, when sitting on a runway, is 55 feet off the ground. When Flight 587 took off from the runway at JFK airport, it weighed 350,000 pounds. It's a huge plane—another reason the limited area of destruction was so remarkable.

The plane's tail broke off and fell into Jamaica Bay, more than a mile from the primary crash site. The engines broke away as well. Falling separately, one landed on Beach 129th Street; the other on Beach 128th. Although a few stray remnants landed here and there, the fuselage and wings pounded into the home on the corner of Beach 131st Street and Newport Avenue. The plane's impact, subsequent explosions, and fire destroyed other homes.

In Belle Harbor, Tom and Helen Concannon, a married couple in their 70's; Frank Pomponio, a husband and father in his 40's; and 48-year-old Kathie Lawler and her 24-year-old son Chris were killed.

It's not fair or wise to measure one death against another, but Chris Lawler's death seemed particularly striking, even inconceivable. It wasn't his age, though he was the youngest person killed on the ground that day. Like Charlie Heeran, who died at the World Trade Center, Chris was another of the local guys who called themselves the RIBs. It was Chris who posted that Internet message to Charlie just weeks before: "I miss you every day, pal."

Chris had been struggling since Charlie's death. Following September 11, Chris missed three straight weeks of law school. By October, he was not really past the sadness but had returned to class. Oddly enough, once he decided to go back, he didn't miss a class—until the morning of November 12.

Although many schools and businesses were closed for the holiday, St. John's Law School was in session, so Chris should have been there. Instead, he stayed in bed and it cost him his life. Two months and a day after Charlie was killed, Chris was dead—killed in much the same manner as Charlie. It would be unusual for two friends to be killed in separate plane crashes had they been flying in those planes. Here, two best pals—two RIBs—were killed because planes struck where they happened to be on separate mornings, two months apart.

■ Monsignor Geraghty has to fend off a number of media people trying to get into the rectory under false pretenses. They try to gain entry with stories about losing family, or claim they're present because of official government business—all in hopes of getting some kind of news scoop. At the same time, he does feel an obligation to address the media about what he knows and about how the people of Rockaway will cope.

First things first. He's like everyone else: he has family and friends outside Rockaway who are desperate to know how he's doing. Of course, on his list, too, is the matter of trying to contact Tom Lawler and others who've lost family members, though he knows there won't be much to say.

■ On television, by early afternoon, they're saying it looks like an accident. A few hours later, a large section of the plane's tail fin is plucked from Jamaica Bay by the Army Corps of Engineers. At the crash site, heavy-duty light stanchions are installed. The digging will go on through the night. Some firefighters, emergency responders, and civilians go to the Harbor Light for a beer.

A joke, a funny line, anything to relieve the stress, is welcome. That's why so many enjoy the story about two civilians helping stretch line—getting a fire hose through the front door of the house on Beach 128th Street where one of the jet engines had crashed.

"I know you're not supposed to laugh at a time like this," one guy says to the other, "but look at that fuckin' guy." A man on the street looks like some comic's idea of a survivalist. The guy is pacing back and forth in white long johns and boots, wielding an ax with a long red handle, with a gas mask hanging from his neck.

■ The phone rings in the McVeigh house at close to 10 PM. It's somebody calling from the firehouse. "It's your last day. What about the meal? You coming in?"

His day started when he thought terrorists were targeting Rockaway. He had told his wife, Pat, to take the kids to the basement. The plane hit four blocks from his house. He'd spent the day putting dead bodies in bags. He'd seen more dead bodies on his last day than he had in the last 20 years combined. Twenty years is a long time to be lucky; no reason to press his luck for another night. He had already delayed retirement because of the attacks of September 11.

"You guys enjoy the meal without me."

He figured he'd stop in next week or the week after, but the next thing he'd be doing with the fire department was handing in his retirement papers the next day.

CHAPTER 8

A Cautious Winter

The crash happened so soon after September 11 that it's compared to a devastating aftershock that sometimes occurs after an earthquake. Still struggling with the deaths of so many of its own, the seaside town was weak and raw when Flight 587 fell. Yet, the town is quick to rally.

Tom Lawler and his daughters move in with his sister-in-law, Ann Marie Greene and her family, just two blocks from the crash site, although he has other options about where to live. Neighborhood people—people he might know by face but were not exactly friends—offer their homes to Lawler. They tell him they'll move to a summer house or a relative's house for as long as necessary.

The day after the plane fell, Katelyn and Jen Lawler, needing clothes, go shopping, and coincidentally run into their teammates and coaches from the Bishop Kearney basketball team who'd gotten together to go shopping themselves—shopping for Katelyn and Jen, that is.

So much food shows up that they have to ask people to stop. More clothes, money, and gifts arrive unbidden—sometimes from friends; sometimes from strangers. People say it's the least they can do—maybe the same comfort will be available for them when they need it.

■ Although numerous people had the same fleeting thought at about the same time, in hindsight, it seems slightly absurd. Terrorists did not target Rockaway because Mike Moran challenged

Osama Bin Laden at a concert. Indeed, the plane may have been brought down by terrorism or sabotage, but simple logic frees Moran of any fault.

It's too much of a stretch to think someone could blow up a plane in mid-air, hoping it would fall in Rockaway as some kind of lesson to the outspoken firefighter. Most people, once they realized that it was a single plane—not two or more planes, or bombs or missiles—that had hit Rockaway, no longer thought about Moran's dare. Plenty never worried in the first place. They remained proud that Moran had told that bastard to kiss his royal Irish ass. *Tell him again, Mike!*

In Belle Harbor, the debate about why there was a crash—terrorism, sabotage, or accident—is secondary to the discussion of good fortune. People talk about where they were, what they thought, and what they did.

Tommy Carroll is a bit embarrassed to see his picture in the newspaper the next day. He had gotten to the scene after much of the fire had been extinguished. He didn't want—and felt he didn't deserve—any attention. When others show him the big centerfold shot of him from behind, holding a length of hose, he immediately downplays his role. "Is my ass that big?"

Many people are the same way: quick to help, quick to deflect praise. You'd say, "Good job!" to someone who got there right away, and he'd say, "No, so-and-so got here before I did." Then so-and-so would say he was just one of many.

Steve Stathis had raced to the scene and recognized a lot of friends pitching in. He didn't know his son, Christian, was on the other side of the flames, getting people out of their houses, until much later that night, when they were just recounting the day. There were probably a lot more people there helping than he'd ever hear about.

Some firefighters say it was an easy job—a "lay-up." Because they fought the fire from the exterior, it was a matter of "surround and drown"—no crawling into basements or down blackened hallways with a dozen doors leading to who knows where.

When others are praised, they say they were just in the right place at the right time to help out. Like Bernie Heeran. He'd lost his son, Charlie, on September 11, yet there was no hesitation for him. He ran to the gas station where the jet engine had fallen, helped there, then ran to the Harbor Light to make sure his sister was all right. Once he saw that she—and the Harbor Light —were spared, he could have understandably remained a spectator. Instead, he charged towards the raging fires, making sure nearby houses were evacuated, grabbing hose line when the engine pulled to the scene. Still, Bernie waves off any praise directed at him. He'll tell you the names of half a dozen others who did more. That's the way it is throughout the town.

The prevailing sentiment is about how much worse things could've been. The question of why it happened pales next to the fact that *it did happen*. Even the Blums and Tom Lawler—who lost Kathie, his high school sweetheart who became his wife, and his son—recognize some good fortune. Two members of the family were killed, but, had the girls, Katelyn and Jennifer, not been at early morning basketball practice, and had Tom Lawler not gone golfing that morning, it would have been worse. It so happens that Kathie Lawler's sister, Mary Ellen, and her family live directly behind the Texaco gas station where the jet engine fell. Had that caused explosions or hit their house instead, November 12 could have been a lot worse for the Blums and the Lawlers.

Tom Lawler and the Heerans can't help but think that Charlie Heeran provided some heavenly intervention in the town he loved so well. There's too much coincidence mixed with a lot of good fortune.

"It was close," Charlie's older brother, Sean, said. "It could have been worse. I think my brother threw us a blessing." Lawler agreed and said that Charlie must've wanted his buddy Chris to join him in heaven.

■ There are unsettling aspects of the manner in which officials and investigators handled the crash of American Airlines Flight 587. Accidents happen, of course. Throughout the 80-year history of commercial aviation, there have been many accidents—a number of which remain baffling or inexplicable. By definition, some accidents will be "unprecedented." Without records or solid past histories to review, surprises and baffling things are sure to happen. New understanding and knowledge, unfortunately, often come after disaster.

To use a simple analogy, you might hold a glass out at arm's length and then drop it to the floor. You know it's going to shatter because you've seen glass break before. With that information, you are able to make assumptions. However, if the glass falls on a soft carpet, it might not shatter at all. From that, you might make different assumptions. If the glass has a solid bottom and hits at a particular angle, it might stay intact, chip, or crack. Experiment enough and you'll determine many possible outcomes of what happens when you drop a glass to the floor.

With aircraft, in a sense, experiments are "live" and ongoing, and they usually occur in uncontrolled environments. Investigators are still learning about "how many ways the glass can break," because it's inherent in the evolution of technology and safety. For instance, until metal fatigue or mechanical failure lead to actual disaster, the predictability of these factors is difficult, and sometimes impossible, to gauge. To an extent, computer models can be used to measure how well aircraft can handle something like stress, but it becomes trickier when other factors are considered. How many miles has the plane logged? Did the plane face severe atmospheric conditions? Did it ever experience harsh landings? Has the general maintenance been satisfactory? These issues will vary from aircraft to aircraft.

Of course, the human part of the equation makes flying somewhat of a crapshoot. Perhaps a plane can take off in below-freezing temperatures, but that's assuming human beings do an adequate job de-icing the wings and so forth. Yes, airlines can present statistics about the relative safety of flying, but human error and/or criminal intent are X factors in the overall equation.

When a major airline crash occurs—particularly when the cause is not apparent—an investigation begins immediately, and can last more than a year before a conclusion or determination of cause is reached. Preliminarily, assuming they were recovered, there will be a review of the flight data recorder and the cockpit's voice recorder ("the black box").

As soon as possible, investigators will review the crew list and passenger manifest. Who made up the crew? How experienced were they? Anything unusual in the backgrounds? As for the passengers, were there any suspected terrorists aboard? Who had access to the aircraft in the hours and days before the flight? In the weeks and months ahead, there will be computer simulation and lab tests, stress tests, and materials analyses. Eyewitness testimony will be gathered and video footage, if available, will be studied. There is much to do.

Often, investigators work by a process of elimination and then make "best guesses" in their conclusions, which will be made public in many months. EgyptAir Flight 990 crashed in October 1999. The final report from the NTSB was issued almost two and one-half years later (in March 2002). In that incident, initial reports suggested that a pilot had brought the plane down in a religious suicide. The final NTSB report reflected the early assumptions, though EgyptAir never accepted the theory or findings. The airline submitted arguments suggesting the pilot may have made evasive maneuvers to avoid military or commercial flights, and those actions coincided with a mechanical malfunction.

The point is that, even after more than two years of investigation, a conclusion can be controversial and unsatisfactory to some. Certainly, a hasty conclusion is sure to provoke extreme controversy and suspicion. Therefore, it struck many people as odd that officials were so quick to deem the crash of Flight 587 an accident.

Marion Blakey, chairperson of the NTSB, said on the day of the crash that "all information we currently have" points to an accident. Information? How much information could they have in half a day? She made her statement although there was no indication that a single piece of checked baggage was screened. There are eyewitnesses saying they saw an explosion in the air. The tail of the plane fell off, then the engines fell off. Has that *ever* happened before?

Retired firefighter Tom Lynch, who was on Rockaway Beach Boulevard taking a morning walk when the plane came down, was immediately alarmed by Blakey's statement. He had seen a small explosion of orange flames burst from the plane and compared it to tossing a match on charcoal soaked with lighter fluid. He barely had time to say, "Holy shit!" before a second, larger eruption of flames consumed the entire right side of the plane.

It's remarkable to some that the NTSB—not the FBI—is the lead agency in the investigation. Obvious questions arise: Will the NTSB recognize criminal intent or even pursue the possibility? Certainly, several eyewitnesses believe the NTSB is either purposely or negligently resisting the idea that the plane was brought down by saboteurs or terrorists. If the NTSB is the lead agency, why is the FBI interviewing some witnesses? Will the FBI provide the information they gather to the NTSB?

After weeks of pursuing the NTSB—and not the other way around—a number of witnesses go to the newspapers with their concerns about the NTSB's seeming indifference to their accounts. Among the witnesses are a recently retired police lieutenant, an FDNY deputy chief and a former firefighter—credible witnesses, it would seem. (The NTSB did not appear particularly interested. The board repeatedly issued statements about eventually getting to eyewitness testimony. The official Web site of the agency says, "All persons who can provide eyewitness testimony about this accident should contact the NTSB through e-mail.")

To many people, it's just too much of a coincidence that a tail fin of a commercial jet fell off on Veteran's Day, just two months and a day after September 11. Clearly, another terrorist attack would have crippled the airline industry, and the U.S. economy would have been dealt a serious, perhaps catastrophic, blow. When the stock market opened 13 minutes after the crash occurred, the Dow Jones plummeted 200 points. It began an ascent immediately after Blakey's statement that the crash appeared to be accidental in nature. Indeed, the public seemed to buy fully into Blakey's initial position; the stock market was up for the week.

At the same time, skepticism and disbelief sprouted in parts of Rockaway, Brooklyn, and other parts of Queens, where eyewitnesses had unimpeded views of the plane as it climbed from JFK airport over Jamaica Bay. Tom Lynch was among those who rushed to the site to assist after seeing the plane burst into flames and nose-dive. He hadn't expected his eyewitness account to be so at odds with the official pronouncements of the NTSB.

"How can they say it was an accident before the flight data recorder had been recovered and before the crash investigation team even showed up? I wasn't the only witness. There's plenty, but they say it was an accident before they even interviewed any of us."

Another witness, just as convinced as Lynch, says, "They float all these ideas, hoping one catches on. First, they said it might be a flock of pelicans that flew into the engine. When was the last time you saw a pelican around here? Then we heard it was wake turbulence. Then it was this composite material—a different material than that which is in most planes. Well, then, why didn't they ground the entire fleet? That would be too expensive. Now it's pilot error. They'd better come up with something good because that tail didn't just fall off."

The crash of Flight 587 was the second deadliest aviation disaster in U.S. history, but it gets relatively scant media attention in the weeks and months that follow. It's a sign of the times, perhaps. In years past, the nightly news would have had regular updates on the continuing investigation, and aviation experts would have been regular visitors on broadcasts. Now, in many places, it's accepted as an accident and the news focus shifts easily to the war in Afghanistan, to new homeland security warning alerts, to Ground Zero updates, to the continuing hunt for Osama Bin Laden.

In Rockaway, it doesn't matter what path the nightly news follows. Witnesses don't necessarily have an opinion about whether it was terrorism or sabotage, or even something mechanical that caused the crash of Flight 587, but they stand by what they saw.

Pete Hayden, who'd been out walking his dog, says, "I don't know the cause. I don't know anything about aviation. But I know smoke and I know fire—and I know when I see a plane blow apart. Again, I don't know what the cause is, but it wasn't turbulence. We see planes take off all the time in Rockaway. My whole life, I've seen them take off. This time, there was a blow-out on the right side."

Another witness, Tom Lynch says, "There were no falling parts until the second explosion of flames—I'll go to my grave with that."

■ Before the crash of Flight 587, it could be said that the only connection between the salt air hamlet of Belle Harbor and the urban air environs of Washington Heights was the A line of the New York City subway system: both places are on near opposite ends of the track.

Washington Heights has apartment buildings, many of them lurching over too-narrow streets. It's also home to more than 150,000 Dominicans; the area is a hotbed of Dominican culture in New York. Belle Harbor is a pleasing mix of Tudors, colonials, and Queen Annes on tree-lined streets. It's home to mostly Irish, Italian Americans and Jews.

Now, the two places are united in grief. At a memorial ceremony held at Riis Park Beach, 4,000 to 5,000 people turn out to remember those killed in the crash just six days before. Monsignor Geraghty speaks and offers prayers to the crowd in English and Spanish.

One of the famed Irish tenors, Ronan Tynan, manages to find something besides grief to unite the divergent groups. To the Dominicans present, he dedicates "Isle of Hope, Isle of Tears"—a song about a 15-year-old Irish immigrant named Annie Moore, who was the first recorded immigrant processed on Ellis Island. The tenor recognizes that so many of the people in the crowd—and those who died on Flight 587—come from an island country to the island of Manhattan with a mix of hope and sorrow, just as Annie Moore and millions of Irish had.

After the ceremony, Dominicans take buses and cars a mile or so east to the crash site. In Belle Harbor, residents line the street between the St. Francis de Sales Church and the crash site. Children and adults hold or solemnly wave small Dominican Republic flags to welcome the mourners to their neighborhood.

■ It's the night before Thanksgiving at the Harbor Light. Charlie Heeran and Chris Lawler were supposed to be behind the bar tonight, serving drinks to a raucous crowd. Instead, they're memorialized on the walls. There's a shot of Charlie smiling in a graduation photo. Opposite the wall, a basketball jersey hangs: it's Chris's Number 12 from Xavier High School.

Thanksgiving is yet another odd day, full of mixed feelings. The crash happened just nine days before. For some, it's an obvious day to feel fortunate and blessed, yet you know that so many families are in particular pain today. Holidays are like that. Christmas might be hardest of all.

Plywood surrounds the crash site. In a way, it's reminiscent of so many firehouses after September 11 as flowers, candles, wreaths, and prayer cards adorn the area. Weeks later, the smell of the fires still hangs in the air. You wonder if it will ever go away.

You hope Tom Lawler has it right at the funeral for his wife and son. He hadn't expected to speak; he didn't want to. Then he sees his daughter, Kate, give the best eulogy, the best speech, he's ever heard. She is so brave.

"We were all family by chance, best friends by choice," she tells the overflow crowd.

What a kid! He'd better get up there, too. He stands at the podium.

"I'm a list kind of guy, whether it's about an upcoming family gathering or a business meeting. Tell me the who, the what, the when, the how, and the where. The who? Well," he says, looking at his kids, "we used to be the Sensational Six. Now we're the Fab Four. The what? We're saying good-bye to people we loved and we're moving on. When? Right now. How? With our families and you, our friends. That's how we'll do it."

The people, the church, the throng on the sidewalk and streets outside burst into applause. If people aren't clapping, they're wiping their eyes.

■ Over the next few months, tiny intangible steps are taken. Scholarship funds are established in Kathie and Chris Lawler's name. The Bishop Kearney basketball team dedicates its season to the Lawlers; the girls wear black armbands during games. Some man reading a newspaper in a Wendy's restaurant in Minnesota reads about the Lawlers and sends a check for $1,000. A woman from upstate New York makes beautiful quilts for all the families who lost their homes. Crews work diligently and unobtrusively to clear the crash site. They seem committed to removing all contamination from any jet fuel that leaked into the ground.

Bernie Heeran gets a phone call from a woman who wants to tell him that Charlie tried to save her daughter when the tower was burning. Her daughter called her on the phone, and told her she was going to be all right and that she was going with Charlie. No one above the plane's impact made it out of the north tower, but Bernie feels better getting confirmation of what he already knew: Charlie died a hero. Even better, his remains are found, so the Heerans give Charlie a funeral mass.

Bernie—his eyes wet, his voice trembling—clenches his fist to gather the strength needed to talk about his son. He's crushed, but grateful, too. He looks out at familiar faces at Xavier High School's chapel. Old friends are the best friends, and new friends become good friends.

■ Bulloch's Texaco station is repaired and reopens. Mike Moran gets married at St. Francis de Sales Church. There are men in kilts and the bagpipes don't sound so sad. Tommy and his guys at Engine 219 and Ladder 105 make a trip to Ground Zero. They touch the last standing beam of the south tower and say good-bye to their fallen brothers.

Matt Tansey strives to get better. Injured, still sad, he's unsure of the future, but feels better with the coming summer sun. His apartment is beautifully fixed; it's more than doubled in value in no time at all. He's bent on doing whatever it takes to get better.

Chief Hayden could retire, but, of course, he can't and won't. He can't leave the job he's loved so much—and he won't now, not after all the losses. He has to make sure the FDNY gets back on its feet, especially at a time when so many firefighters will be leaving. Many have financial incentive to retire.

A firefighter's pension, which retired firefighters receive immediately upon leaving the job, is based on a firefighter's highest earning year. With all the overtime accumulated in the aftermath of September 11, many firefighters know it would be fiscally irresponsible to stay on the job. In simple terms, it will cost them money to stay.

Hayden can't argue with that—they have to take care of their families—but he also knows many of them will have a hard time leaving the firehouse. He's seen it before. All those years, fighting fires together, sharing sleeping quarters, enjoying the big meals. The stuff about the fire department being a second family is all too true. For a lot of guys, it'll be difficult to walk away.

A high percentage of the remaining firefighters will have six years or less on the job. Pete Hayden and a handful of others will have a say in how the FDNY moves forward. So, he'll stick around. The job—the laughs, the deep bonds, the guys. He'd do it all over again in a second.

■ Bishop Kearney, an all-girls high school, is across the bridge in Brooklyn. Its basketball team is stamped with the Rockaway seal. Four of the five starters come from The Rock and so does the team's coach, Cathy Crockett. There are so many "Kates" on the team that the players call each other by their last names.

They won a bunch of games as they rode an emotional wave after the plane crash, after they had dedicated the season to Kathie and Chris Lawler, but they couldn't sustain it over the long season. By late January, the team started to struggle. They lost once, then again. Soon they were slumping badly enough that one more loss would end their season, killing any chance of competing in the New York State playoffs.

With about two minutes to go in a game that looked like it would end the season and the career of senior Katelyn Lawler, a sophomore by the name of Jen Lawler hit a big three-point shot, giving Kearney the lead for good. The shot not only helped win the game but also marked the start of an amazing turnaround. Suddenly, they could run faster, shoot better. They could see the open man on offense and smother a team on defense. In the final four of the "C" division playoffs, they rolled past a big team from Buffalo, then easily beat another school for the state title.

Parents, coaches, and players all stood around, grinning like fools. A few weeks earlier, the state title was so unlikely that now there was nothing to do but grin. It felt so right. Coach Cathy Crockett said, "Let's celebrate at the Harbor Light!"

There was hot food in the front room and a deejay in the back. The girls started dancing almost immediately, forming a circle with their arms around each other, singing to all the songs. The parents and coaches got choked up looking at the girls—something so triumphant about them belting out bar anthems after all they'd been through. When they sung *We're magic! We're magic!* from "Celtic Symphony," it was time to get drunk.

Some parents and a couple of firefighters—Vinny O'Grady and Keith Green, who happened to be married to two of the coaches—hit the dance floor and the party was on. Someone got some chairs into a semicircle, and the girls stood on them to resume singing their bar standards. When "We Are Family!" started, one of the fathers jumped into the middle of the chairs and started belting along.

Then Tom Lawler climbed up on a chair, and the two of them stood in the middle of the girls, arms around each other, belting out *"We Are Fam-i-ly"* for all it was worth. Vinny, Keith, the coaches, and all the players joined in, arms interlocked, singing it with the right mixture of defiance and triumph.

In Rockaway, in the Harbor Light.

CHAPTER 9

Rockaway Rises Again

In Rockaway, landmarks are like sand castles. They're short-lived, full of fleeting beauty, too vulnerable to the elements. So much of old Rockaway, built on wood, continues to disappear. Just six months after the crash of Flight 587, Derech Emunoh—the Georgian style synagogue built in 1904—burned to the ground.

There was a familiar lament as 140 firefighters using 33 pieces of equipment battled the blaze ripping through the big, brown shingled structure: wood and wind. Bad electrical wiring might have started the fire, but the wood frame and the gusty wind gave the fire the potency it needed to destroy the building that had long cast shadows over vacant lots.

It was a sad ending to the impressive building that had seen its congregation shrink to fewer than 50 people. Particularly sad because it had rebounded from arson attacks in 1994 and 1995—a man was convicted and was serving time when the final fire raged. Particularly sad because there was renewed hope that the congregation would grow. New houses and new developments were starting to fill the vacant lots that stretched into an overgrown wasteland since Mayor Lindsay and Robert Moses crippled Rockaway in the 1960s.

Another landmark is gone, but fire and urban planners can only do so much to Rockaway because, as someone said at the scene, "It's a shame losing a building, but if there's anything that marks this place, it's the people. They're tough, with the ocean nearby; they've got a lot of salt in them."

∎ The crowds came back with Memorial Day, just a couple of weeks ago. The beaches will be packed until Labor Day.

Billy and Sean Heeran wait for the doors of the A train to open. The slow, sweaty ride from Wall Street doesn't bother either of them all that much. It's not as if they'd be doing it forever. They step out onto Beach 116th Street, just as their brother, Charlie, had done nine long months ago. A steady crush of DFDs, coming from the beach, hurry past them to the train. The air is filled with coconut oil and beer. A bald-headed fat man—with a mesh tank top, bikini-style bathing suit, and black shoes and socks—pushes a curly-haired kid in a stroller.

Three teenage girls, looking over their shoulders and laughing, run into the subway station. Three boys, trying to be cool, follow them a few seconds later. A guy on crutches passes—he has one leg, and the long, bell-bottomed pants leg that falls free flaps in the breeze behind him. He goes into a liquor store.

The red doors of the firehouse across the street slide upward. Kenny Whelan, the captain, wears navy blue shorts and an FDNY polo shirt—perfect attire for this time of year, especially at the firehouse they call The Beach House. He stands to the side as a fire truck rolls slowly out of the garage, a banana-yellow rescue surfboard fastened to its side. Billy and Sean glance at each other, both feeling the same jolt of pride when they see the bright red letters on the surfboard: Rockapulco.

A small whirlwind spins Styrofoam cups and loose papers around their feet as they step into a warm, offshore wind. Cigarette butts and small clusters of sand bounce past them as they push their way towards the ocean boardwalk. Billy loosens his tie and puts his hands in the pockets of his light pin-striped suit. The bus stop is crowded with people wondering if the bus will ever come. A dollar store has expanded, and sells cheap sunglasses and flip-flops from sidewalk tables. A cop is checking parking meters.

They think about stopping for a cold one at the tiki bar set up outside The Beach Club, but, if they have one, that might lead to two. They'd better not. Billy has to bartend at the Harbor Light in a couple of hours—a bit more serious gig now that he and Sean had become partners with their dad in May. It was going to be great—though it would never be the same without Charlie. All the plans, the personality of the place—everything would have revolved around Charlie.

The boardwalk planks are loose, some raised just enough to make you trip. Baby waves break right at the shoreline. A few blocks west, a bunch of kids—maybe 12 or 13 years old—are playing baseball in the sand. They are using a whiffle ball bat and tennis ball. It looks like they are having a blast.

Sean points to the kids in the sand and nods. It's shorthand for, that's what life is. Rockaway. He grew up here. His kids, when he has a family, will grow up here, too. He works in Manhattan, even has a place in the city. But Rockaway? You couldn't beat it.

They both sling their jackets over their shoulders. A man and his wife or girlfriend on bicycles nod at them as they pass. The man is wearing a familiar gray T-shirt with raised white letters on the front: "Rockaway, It's Not Just A Beach"; on the back: "It's A Lifestyle."

The ocean looks like a lake. A sand bar a few hundred yards offshore causes a few ripples, but otherwise the water is smooth, almost cobalt blue. Sandy Hook, New Jersey seems close enough to touch. A cruise ship, heading into the New York Harbor, looks like a wedding cake.

They turn off the boardwalk at Beach 126th Street. Before they get to Rockaway Beach Boulevard, they hear a referee's whistle from the schoolyard two blocks over. The sound means that games are being played in the Summer Classic—the basketball league enjoyed by just about everyone from second graders to Graybeards, the over-40 crowd.

■ Two picnic tables are pushed together end to end, so that the McVeighs, Carrolls, and Kellehers can sit together. The early summer washes over them like a seasonal baptism. When beers are served, they clink bottles in a good-luck toast. It isn't exactly a birthday party, but Tommy is calling it one.

"What? You guys aren't gonna sing 'Happy Birthday'?" Tommy asks.

"Please, it's next week," Eileen says.

"This year, my birthday's like Chanukah. I'm celebrating tonight and then for eight more days."

It feels good to be back at The Wharf—a place they don't see from October to May. McVeigh tells Tommy he has to buy the first round. "Happy birthday. Now buy the first round. You're getting the tuition break."

T.J.—Tommy and Eileen's son—was awarded an academic scholarship to Xavier High School. T.J. and 11 other kids from Rockaway, including the McVeigh's son, would start freshman year at Xavier in September, keeping the pipeline strong.

"No, no, no. You're buying 'cause you can afford to pay my kid's tuition, your kid's tuition, that kid's tuition over there. You're a suit now."

Happy Jack Driscoll, at another table, says they're both cheap bastards.

Inside, Whipper Stathis is at his second job, tending bar, talking to his brother, Steve, who is wearing a Rockaway Graybeard shirt with a logo, "Old Maybe, But Not Extinct." Steve is saying the Graybeards, now a group dedicated more to community service than to basketball, has more than 80 members, and new guys are trying to join all the time.

It's 8:30 PM and there's still at least 20 minutes before the sun drops out of sight.

"So, really, how's work?" Tommy Carroll asks McVeigh about his new life as an executive with a moving company.

"Good. I think I'm finally getting used to it."

"It's tough without those mutuals," Tommy offers.

"It is, it is. Regular nine to five after 20 years. It is tough. Pretty soon, you'll see," McVeigh says.

"Nah, once I retire from the fire department, I'll probably stick with construction."

"Would you work at the Trade Center site?"

"Sure, why not? It'd be great to have a hand in the memorial they're gonna build. Somehow."

The official end of the clean-up and recovery phase at Ground Zero had occurred at the end of May, months ahead of what was expected. Of the more than 2,800 people killed in the attack, just 1,102 had been identified. Nearly 20,000 body parts had been recovered. More remains would be identified through DNA analysis and there would certainly be more funerals. Rebuilding would start soon, and the hope was that a suitable memorial would rise from the ashes and dust.

Steve stops at the table, says hello to everyone, then reminds Kevin Kelleher that they have a game tomorrow morning. The Graybeards basketball season is a few weeks old.

Happy Jack Driscoll, three tables over, somehow hears the conversation and can't resist. "His team sucks. And he sucks."

Everyone laughs. There goes Jack. Good, old predictable Jack.

"Some things never change."

It's a simple statement that turns everyone pensive for a moment, because some things do change. Like the view from the deck of The Wharf. It's a cloudless blue sky, and the sunset's going to be a beauty, but the view and sunset aren't quite the same without the Twin Towers.

"It's still beautiful," Eileen says.

▪ Full-court games are underway on each of the four courts in the St. Francis schoolyard. Grade-school kids in pastel-colored T-shirts shoot or guard each other tightly; some make sharp cuts and set picks. The coaches cheer them on, telling them to find the open man. When the kids hustle back on defense, the coaches urge them to help out. Parents pack the temporary bleachers set up along each court. Dozens of people on the sidewalk watch the action through the schoolyard's cyclone fence.

The Summer Classic is more than a tradition. It's simply one of the best things about the summer in Rockaway. There's good basketball action, but it's the town square, too. You see people you haven't seen all winter. The Classic gives the community an undeniable jolt of renewal. It's been that way for nearly 20 years—ever since Bernie Heeran, Bugsy Goldberg, Flip Mullen, and Steve Stathis formed the league so kids would have something to do in the summer, after a day on the beach.

It's easy for Billy and Sean to spot Ryan Whelan. He's wearing a black-and-white striped shirt, refereeing a game. Like father, like son. In an hour or so, Kenny Whelan will cycle home from the firehouse and be on the court with a whistle for the Men's Open league.

George Johnson drives past in his car, looking a little distracted. Billy wonders if he'll be going to the rugby tournament tomorrow. Probably not. The captain's test is next week.

Tom Lawler's in the crowd, watching a game with his sister-in-law, Ann Marie Greene, and her husband. Right next to him, his goddaughter K.C.—named for Kathie and Chris—is being rocked in a stroller by Kathie's cousin, Ellen. All that coaching and cheering for his daughter Katelyn had paid off. Not only did her team go out as champs, she was named playoff Most Valuable Player and then surpassed all expectations by making the All-City team. The Lawlers have just bought a new home on a beach block around the corner from Ann Marie, across the street from Flip Mullen.

Palmer Doyle is watching a game, too. It looks like he's just come from coaching a Little League game; he's got baseball diamond dirt around his ankles.

Monsignor Geraghty is sharing small talk and laughs with some parents. He doesn't mind that small kids are using him as a shield in a game of tag.

■ The Heeran brothers cross Newport Avenue—the Harbor Light is to their left. The house on the corner, directly across the street from the pub, is still charred and surrounded by plywood. So is the house directly behind that one, on Beach 131st Street.

Yet, there is less and less tangible evidence that a plane—a 350,000-pound, 177 feet in length behemoth—crashed here. For the time being, a large, manicured lawn covers the area where the homes of the Concannons, Lawlers, and Pomponios once stood. The street is newly paved; another house damaged by fire is being restored. The neighborhood's physical scar continues to shrink and fade.

Billy takes off his tie and stuffs it in the pocket of his suit jacket. He's always loved the summer in Rockaway, but, in one way, he couldn't wait for this one to end. Then his life would really start.

Sean jogs up the front steps of the Harbor Light. He'd been breaking his back on Wall Street for five years. Things were starting to come together. He'd soon be making the money he dreamed about—though that dream didn't have that much appeal any longer. Now, a new dream was taking form. He didn't know when, but he knew he'd have to make a tough decision when the call finally came.

Billy heads around back, glancing back at Sean as he goes up the steps and inside. His buddy, Pete Hayden, Jr., the chief's son, sits on a flimsy chair handling the valet parking—a needed position with the summer parking restrictions in effect.

They slap hands hello. Billy gives him a look. "I can't wait."

Pete nods. "Me, too."

As soon as the summer was over, Billy was giving up the job on Wall Street. Pete would no longer be an emergency medical technician. They'd be both answering the call. Like their fathers before them, both of them would be entering the Fire Academy.

▪ As the final buzzer sounds for the games in the schoolyard, 20 or 30 kids run for their bicycles lined up along the fence, then speed out—some go home, some go to Papa's Pizza down the block. Adults in long-sleeved T-shirts and shorts file out. There are easy laughs amidst talk about the next game, barbecues, and upcoming weddings. Somebody says there is supposed to be great beach weather tomorrow. It seems like a good possibility because the sky is clear and the wind feels soft and cool. Some say they are going to stop at the Harbor Light for a beer, or maybe two, then head around the corner to Jamesons.

Lights from the schoolyard and from the church across the street shine down on the sidewalk. It's like Tom Lawler said at the double funeral for Kathie and Chris. In his impromptu eulogy, he gave his list of who, what, when, how. And as for the where? Well, he said, his daughters were worried that he'd want to move away after the plane crash, that he'd take them somewhere to start new lives.

Where are we going to live? they wanted to know.

He paused just a bit, and set his eyes on everyone. "Where else but Rockapulco?"

Biographies

Tommy Carroll, 42, has been a firefighter for 17 years for Engine 219, Ladder 105 in Brooklyn. He is married to Eileen and has three children: T.J., Brianne, and Sean.

Palmer Doyle, 48, has been a firefighter for 14 years for Engine 254 in Brooklyn. He is married and the father of two.

Monsignor Martin Geraghty, 61, has been pastor of St. Francis de Sales Church in Belle Harbor, Rockaway for 13 years.

Pete Hayden, 54, climbed the ranks with the Fire Department of New York (FDNY) for 34 years. On September 11, he was deputy chief and division commander (Manhattan). He was in charge of the North Tower Command/Operations post. Two months later, on his first day off from work, he witnessed Flight 587 explode in the air and crash into his neighborhood. He was senior FDNY officer on the scene. He is married to Rita and they have five children. His brother, Jack, is a firefighter; his son, Pete, Jr., is with the Emergency Medical Service division of the FDNY.

The Heerans: Bernie Heeran, 54, is a retired firefighter (Engine 281 in Brooklyn). He owns the Harbor Light restaurant in Belle Harbor, Rockaway. He is the father of five. He steered his three sons—oldest Sean, and twins Charlie and Billy, 23—away from the firefighting life because he considered it too dangerous. They each had Wall Street jobs (though they all took the FDNY exam). Charlie, also a rugby player, would one day run the Harbor Light. On September 11, he was an equities trader for Cantor Fitzgerald, and had recently declined an opportunity to work in London. He, like Sean and Billy, are part of a neighborhood bunch who called themselves the RIBs (Rockaway Irish Boys).

George Johnson, 38, is single, a surfer, a former lifeguard, and a firefighter for 11 years for Ladder 157 in Brooklyn. He is one of the three flag-raising firefighters. His father, George, Sr., is a retired FDNY captain; his brothers Bob and Mike are firefighters as well.

The Lawlers: Tom, 48; Kathie, 48, his high school sweetheart. Their children are Chris, 24, Brendan, Katelyn, and Jennifer. Chris, a law student, is an RIB and a buddy of Charlie Heeran. Tom is a manager at the Federal Reserve, and a basketball coach and fan.

Tom McVeigh, 42, was due to retire from the FDNY in late September 2001 and stayed on for two more months. His last scheduled day of work is November 12—the day Flight 587 crashed just a few hundred yards from his home. He is married to Pat; their children are Sean and Kaitlyn.

Flip Mullen, 57, is a retired firefighter. He is married to Rita, and they have seven children. He managed to get into lower Manhattan on the back of a motorcycle on September 11.

Steve Stathis, 52, is a Con Edison emergency response team member. He is married and the father of three. His brother Peter (Whipper) and son Christian are with the FDNY. Steve started the community-based, nonprofit group called the Graybeards.

Whipper Stathis, 45, is a firefighter, a surfer, and responded on September 11 and to the plane crash. He is the brother of Steve.

Matt Tansey, 27, is single, a former lifeguard, and a firefighter for five years for Ladder 12 in Manhattan. He agreed to work on September 11 for another firefighter.

Kenny Whelan, 48, is captain of Ladder 137 on Beach 116th Street in Rockaway. He is married to Roseanne, and is the father of Ryan, an RIB.